# GINGER

## A Boy's Journey from Scotland to the White House

By David T. Macfarlane

**DUNROBIN PUBLISHING**

www.dunrobin.us

Permission to quote in critical reviews with citation:
*GINGER*
By David T. Macfarlane

For permission to reproduce contact:
Dunrobin Publishing
www.dunrobin.us
permissions@dunrobin.us


ISBN 978-0-9832363-7-5

www.dunrobin.us

Dedicated to my wife Christina.


Without your support this book would never have been.

# FOREWORD

My story. The story of a boy, who was born and raised in Scotland, and who moved to the United States at age 10. The product of an immigrant family where a new life, divorce, alcoholism, poverty and desire drive this boy to become an award winning chef-- overcoming a situation where all the odds are against him. From the streets of New Jersey to being hand picked to cook at the White House for the President of the United States.

Ginger is not by any means a sad story. To the contrary, it is about passion for a career that would separate the man from the boy. From shy and insecure to a driven, fanatical perfectionist trying to learn from the past and wish it was different—only to come to terms with what really matters and the things that cannot be changed.

Ginger is a boy who never gave up. A boy that never accepted life's trials and misgivings as an excuse to give in and accept uncontrollable conditions that shape one's life for the worse. His will is not hereditary but is instead contrary to his father's will.

You might think that when people move to another country, life would be easier upon acclimation. In reflection, nothing could be further from the truth. For Ginger's family, this move was not easy. His social class would be transformed from what he perceived as normal, happy and content to abnormal, unhappy and discontent.

Life, as you may know, is only easy if you are living somebody else's and never your own. If someone else has planned it for you and paid your way through the tolls of adversity then yes, life is easy.

i

This homesick boy learns to adjust and start a new life. Unfortunately, not a better life but rather one that challenges him to be a better person in the end and not to be fooled by not being good enough to do what makes him happy.

He's a boy who wants to be a chef and he does just that. He doesn't settle for an easy occupation, as a result of a hard life, but rather one that takes hard work, dedication and the ability to please people and wanting nothing in return. It's an occupation that is never glamorous. It is hot, uncomfortable, and stressful and drives the sane to be insane.

Ginger becomes an artist in a craft that relishes taking in the castaways of normal society and exploiting them for their mere self gratification and addictions, only to pay them with the pains of hardship. But it is love and love is blind.

This is not a cookbook; this is a cook's book. This is my book.

# SALUTE

With an uncontrollable desire to be a chef, my career started with having to learn to prepare meals at home with minimal ingredients and maximum results to feed a family of six. It wasn't the fancy French foods that drew me into cooking. It wasn't clinging to anybody's apron strings as a child and being nurtured in a kitchen filled with love. It was the necessity of sustainable nourishment with extremely limited money that made me creative and planted the seed of cookery in the soil of my brain, with my heart and soul to follow.

Was it my Scottish ingenuity that kicked in to make a meal out of nothing? Quite possibly. The Scots have a reputation for frugal living but so does every culture outside of the US, the land of plenty, where frugal practices have engineered a world of gastronomy marvels. The Scots are just entertaining about being thrifty but, reality is, I am Scottish and maybe, just maybe, within my inherent DNA, through a thousand years of my ancestors' inability to afford to waste, is the ability to create anything out of nothing from a culture never to be heralded for its food. Yet.

Turns out, Scottish food is delicious. It ranks up there, in my book, with classical French cookery. And because of the use of discarded, peasant parts of animals, and stews or soups created by what is on hand and not with "what do I need to get at the shops?", our foods are not that much different. Every mise en place (ingredient) list should always start with imagination and finish with perfection.

As a child, eating was never really pleasurable. It was unintentionally disconnected from my core being and never regarded

iii

as soulful until later in life when I could connect foods with memories. Whether good or bad, I needed an association of the two to truly realize what I liked and disliked. Take beef for example. I hated it as a child but later I found that it wasn't the beef I hated but rather the preparation that prevented me from liking it. This memory is a fond memory, not a bad one, even though the beef was bad.

Scottish cuisine lacked, and still does, a romance with its food the way the French romance about theirs. And placing technique at the forefront of preparation with a flair for using French wines was pure genius.

Italian culture taught me to be passionate about food. No matter your mood, your finances, your restrictions or your lack of knowledge, Italian cooking is simple. That is what makes it so good. Once you perfect how to make pasta then you can perfect how to cook it with other ingredients, perfect how to make the breads to accompany it and perfect how to season the foods with herbs and wines instead of ketchup or just salt.

I owe an incredible debt of gratitude to the Italian culture for showing me passion for food. Something no school, whatever the cost, can teach.

Just as music can have an impact on your emotions, I want to have an emotional impact through my cooking. Just like when you hear a certain song or score that brings out an emotion or a memory, that makes you happy, sad, loved or lonely, it is my desire to do the same with food.

All the people in this book, along with many different forms of artists, some of whom I have never met, influenced my life in many ways whether it be good or bad.

A formal education was out of the question since the cost was unrealistic, in my opinion, and kept me from learning in the conventional way. I had to learn in what would be the unconventional way, by today's standard, by means of 'on the job training,' until joining the US Navy for an education that I otherwise could not afford.

I started to not only learn the foods of other cultures but more so the cultures themselves. Why do they eat this? Why do they prepare it this way? Understanding not just the food but the people who prepare it will immerse you in understanding why things are the way they are.

If Japanese culture wasn't so disciplined and driven to perfection, would their foods reflect an undisciplined and mediocre culture. Of course so. It is the goal to be perfect that makes it perfect. Perfect cuts, perfect preparation and perfect presentation are all derived from the culture. The ingredients are made from what's available and the tools used for preparation are made of the same.

To have a relationship with food is to have a relationship that can give back what you put into it. If you love it, it will love you back. Very few things in life do this. I can love my car but it loves the mechanic's shop more. The love that is returned to me from food is the happiness that touches whoever partakes. Whether it be my family, my guests or my customers. If they are happy, then so am I. Learning how to do so never came easy to me. I had to work hard at it. I never regarded myself as self taught. It was always someone or something that I learned from.

Planning goes a long way into making a relationship work. The same goes for cooking. Planning is to learn the art and learn it well in order to execute what it is you want to accomplish. Wisdom only comes with knowledge. To plan a meal or a menu, you must know what you want the outcome to be before the preparation even begins. Do you want it to be enjoyed? Do you want it to be trendy, artistic or crave-able? How you approach the meal is how your knowledge determines the outcome.

GINGER

# WORLDS APART

It was a very snowy and cold night at John F. Kennedy airport in the early morning hours of February 19, 1978, when this 10-year-old arrived in America from Scotland.

A move that I wasn't too excited about but one I thought of as an adventure. This was my first time out of the United Kingdom, as well as my first time on an airplane. I must admit that I was more excited than nervous but didn't know what to expect or what it would be like to travel across the Atlantic at around 450 miles per hour at an altitude of around 32,000 feet. Thankfully, the plane was half empty so we had plenty of room on the DC-10 wide body with its four seats across the middle and three at each window.

We flew from London Gatwick, to New York aboard the Laker Skytrain, a low-cost, no-frills airline that was the brainchild of Sir Freddy Laker. Tickets were sold in train stations with no need for middlemen travel agents adding unnecessary cost. At the time, it revolutionized the way people travelled by air because of the bare bones approach to air travel. Was this a sign of things to come? Absolutely!

The first thing I noticed upon boarding was the weird orange pattern that the seats were upholstered in. Even though it was the 1970s, I did not expect a color scheme that was so out of the ordinary. Almost a paisley pattern of bright orange and white with a white head rest cover Velcro-attached to the top of the seat. The carpet was a darker burnt orange color and, being a small boy who was around 50 lbs soaking wet, the seats had plenty of room. We were sitting in the smoking section so Mum and Dad could smoke and each hand rest had its own ashtray built in, which I thought was pretty cool.

I can't remember the movie that was played on the 8-hour trip since Sir Freddy sold the headsets for $2 each and we were not going to be getting any entertainment expenses covered. So we did our best to entertain ourselves with coloring books and whatever else we could find in our bags.

Now, I understand how difficult it must have been for both of my parents to make such a dramatic change with five children, even if it meant getting there at the absolute lowest cost. Knowing my father, if he could have gotten away with smuggling us in bags he would have certainly done so with no remorse. My parents didn't even buy any meals for us on our 8-hour journey in an effort to save money but they had their fags (cigarettes) to keep them happy and they didn't seem bothered that we had nothing to eat. But this was the norm that we were used to. The flight attendant felt so sorry for us that she offered to give us some leftover meals that Sir Freddy couldn't sell to the thrifty punters on their way to the opportune shores of the U.S. of A.

Of course my parents obliged. Probably anything to shut us up. Again, another sign that things were changing for the worse? You bet!

We waited at the airport for my Uncle Tommy to pick us up. He lived in New Jersey. He was my father's older brother, as well as his only brother. I had never met him before nor had any of my sisters, but he turned out to be very kind to us and we were all very glad to meet and get to know him since we learned he was nothing like his brother.

The first memory I have about arriving in America was seeing a hand gun for the very first time in my life. A cop at the airport was walking around where we were waiting for my uncle to pick us up. What stands out most was how sloppy he looked. He was wearing his cap all the way back on his head so as to cover the back and not the top. His shirt was loosely tucked in and his gun was in a cowboy style holster halfway down his thigh. So far down that it was visible even when he was wearing his leather winter jacket. I couldn't believe the fact that I was seeing a gun, but his appearance caught me as odd as if he had nobody to answer to by looking so unprofessional but maybe that is just how it was. I guess I would assume more self pride, especially when carrying a gun that is simply used to demand respect and quite possibly put an end to someone's life. But all I knew about American police is what I saw on television, so to see one for real was really quite disappointing.

The police back home were always very sharply dressed and carried themselves with important pride. They are very official looking and very respectful. Even though they did not carry a gun you still got scared when they would approach you just because of their demeanor and very polished, almost rehearsed, way of speaking.

My uncle finally arrived and before we knew it the car was loaded and we were on our way to New Jersey. Now my father had been to the U.S. the previous month in order to make arrangements for our accommodation upon arrival but it was not ready, for some reason, so we ended up spending a few weeks with Uncle Tommy and his family in North Arlington. When we arrived at his house we unloaded the car and fell right to sleep. I would have to wait until the next day before exploring my new surroundings and gauging what exactly I was in for.

The next morning I went outside to check things out. I had never seen that much snow before in my life. The piles on the sidewalk were taller than me. Apparently there was a huge snow storm the past few days but I couldn't believe how much there was. We hardly ever got snow back in East Kilbride. A light dusting usually around the end of November then again in December and that was usually it. This was unbelievable, especially since I was expecting warmer weather in America since it was further south than Scotland. It was freezing. Even though it was sunny I was still the coldest I think I had ever been in my life.

As I walked down the block, not too far since I had no idea where I was, I noticed that cars were huge, houses were huge and I still couldn't believe how much snow there was. Each day I would venture a little further. Sort of an adventure was how I would look at it. My uncle's house was two blocks from the main street and that is where I started from. Sometimes one of my sisters, Catherine or Lauren, would go with me but most of the time I would be alone. I would just look into each shop window as I walked along noticing landmarks to gauge my bearings. The roads were wide I thought, even with a ton of snow all around, and I still couldn't get over how cold it was.

As a kid, I was always fascinated with airplanes and just to the south of us was Newark Airport, so there were planes flying overhead about every five minutes it seemed. I had never seen so much traffic, either on the road or from the air. Asides from my own first flight, I had only seen airplanes twice before and that was when my Mum and older sister, Lauren, went to America in 1976 for a holiday or when my grandfather went to Michigan on holiday. Both times we drove to Prestwick Airport, which seemed like the other side of Scotland at the time. But I loved the drive through the hill country and loved seeing the Atlantic Ocean from the airport observation area. It was great.

I would avoid contact with others as much as possible when I went out, simply because I did not want to explain myself to anyone for talking so differently but primarily because I wasn't ready to interact with people whom, under first impression, I didn't like. Even though this was all new and I was kind of excited about experiencing something different, I really missed home. Especially since this was the first time I had never lived in our own home. For me, this was very uncomfortable and that feeling overshadowed all my other feelings. I was slowly becoming tired of the situation and was anxious to move into our own house, especially since the ones I was seeing while out on my adventures were huge and I would love to have had my own bedroom, having never had one before all to myself. Besides, I had never seen houses this big before in my life. With a family of seven, I thought we would certainly need one of these big houses since everybody else had one.

I would do my best to be out of the way from others especially when school got out. I would usually just stand to the side in a shop doorway or somewhere off the main route and watch the kids as they would walk by. I would try to pick up on what they were wearing, saying and how they were acting. I considered myself quite quiet most of the time but still a normal 10 year old boy that acts the fool when with my friends or playing football (soccer) or spending the day out.

What I saw, from watching the American kids getting out of school, was that everybody wore blue jeans, had long hair and seemed very loud when they spoke. Almost as if they were talking to each other from opposite sides of the street. It would not be until much later when I would leave New Jersey that I would realize that being loud and obnoxious wasn't an American trait but really just one in New Jersey. Each time when I am back to New Jersey, to visit, it is still one thing to this day that stands out most to me and this is something that I never really cared for.

Now, while staying at my uncle's, we ate very much how we ate back home in Scotland. Mince and potatoes, fish, jam sandwiches and plenty of hot tea to drink. I didn't know what to expect from the food in America since the only thing I ever had was Kentucky Fried Chicken back home and as far as I knew that was as American as you could get.

We would pile in the car in East Kilbride and drive for what seemed like ages once a year and pick up Kentucky Fried Chicken. I thought it smelled divine and tasted even better. It was torture having to ride all the way back home and none of us could open this bucket of finger licking goodness until we got home. And to add to the torture my parents would smoke their cigarettes in the car with the windows rolled completely up and our eyes would burn out of our head. All I would think about is how great the bucket of chicken smells and tasting this will be well worth the gas chamber treatment that made you wish it wasn't raining so they would spare us permanent lung damage. But no rain? Scotland? Hardly! I got so sick of that stuff that I ended up opting out of family car trips for food and would stay home

6

or be out with my friends on purpose missing them loading the kids into the car and I am sure they were happy with a lighter load without me.

Italian food and sandwich shops were the predominant food in North Arlington. I had no interest in trying them since I was a very finicky eater and the smell of foreign foods turned me completely off from eating. I missed my meat pies, chips and Irn Bru.

And most of all I missed home.

# FROM WHENCE I COME

I was born at Thornhill Royal Hospital in Elderslie, Scotland, on November 29, 1967. My parents, at the time, were living in a flat in the Mary Hill section of Glasgow. Mary Hill is where my father's family is from and where his mother Nellie owned a shop, as well as offer up reading palms or tea leaves for a few quid on the side. In Scotland it is everyone's second nature to make something on the side. That is our survivor mode which makes us so imaginative as well as resourceful, since regular jobs never seem to pay enough. My older sister Lauren was born in the same hospital 2 years earlier. We lived in a council tenement in Mary Hill. A council home is government provided housing for low income or un-self sustaining wards of the council who pay little or no rent depending upon your income.

My father's income was always sporadic due to him changing jobs more often than normal. It never occurred to me why until my early teens, when I realized he was a full blown alcoholic. Only then did I recognize why things were the way they were and how his behavior was always odd and most of the time embarrassing. As I mentioned earlier, it is common for the Scottish to somehow make some side money and for my father theft was his way of getting by. He would steal anything that wasn't nailed down. My mother told me the story of when they were first married and they were visiting her brothers in Port Glasgow, where she is from. As they left her brothers' flat to head to the pub, one of my father's favorite things to do, he walked back saying he forgot something at her brothers' flat. He met up with them a few minutes later at the pub and then after returning to her brothers' flat they noticed the door window smashed in and the power box broken off the wall. The power box is a coin receptacle that provides electricity to the flat after you deposit money into like a parking meter. When you deposit money into it you get electricity for the value of the deposit. Well, it looked like your standard smash and grab, and all indications pointed to my father as the culprit. My mother says she defended him but didn't realize this was how he operated until years later.

My father was a very sneaky man who was never to be trusted. He was only happy when drinking and always liked to play the big shot. He would buy drinks for strangers, yet never provide the basic necessities for his family. He thought very highly of himself and always made sure his needs were met first. To this day, I do not like ice cream because of my father. Whenever, which was very rare, we would have ice cream after supper he would cut small pieces out of the package for us children then cut a huge piece for himself. He was very greedy and selfish and the ice cream was a prime example. We would all resent him for this and forget to be grateful for what we got, instead becoming envious for what we didn't get.

Human nature I guessed, but more disappointing was his lack of caring. He never let me down in that department. Being disappointed in him is my fondest memories of him.

I have four sisters. Lauren, Catherine, Joanne and Carole. As our family grew it was obvious that my parents needed a bigger house. A flat in Glasgow just wasn't big enough so it was necessary to find something more accommodating but, more importantly, one that was owned by the council.

We ended up moving to the town of East Kilbride. East Kilbride was known at the time as a new town. Meaning it was a planned community that was built 7 miles outside of Glasgow and built with three industrial parks providing jobs for the new community. The local council had brand new houses built in the Green Hills section and the Macfarlanes were taking full advantage of the new opportunity.

Our house was brand new and had plenty of room for all of us. My Mum was pregnant with our youngest sister when we moved in just in time for the window putty to still be moist and not fully set. Dust was everywhere and the floors were still bare. We were all very excited, especially us kids, since now we had a yard to play in and lots of other families moving in each week meant there was a ton of others kids to meet and play with.

Soon after we moved in, my grandfather moved in with us also. At first, I was sharing one of the bedrooms upstairs with my sister Catherine and we had bunk beds to sleep in. There was an extra room downstairs that we used for a dining room that would soon become my grandfather's room but until we got his stuff from Glasgow he stayed with me and slept in the lower bunk bed and Catherine moved to another bedroom.

My grandfather was nothing like my father. Actually, I don't know why he moved in with us since after my grandmother died he moved into one of the high rise flats in Mary Hill. But I wasn't complaining. I really liked him and we became great friends during our time together. To this day I treasure that time. Most of all, I now had someone to admire and look up to. My father never fit that bill and

11

even though I tried he would always find a way to distance himself from me.

Every morning my grandfather would bump his head on the bottom of my bed when he would get up. I thought it was so funny. He never acted like I bothered him but I am sure I did. I was just starting school and he would always check me over before heading out the door. "Dae ya hiv yer books?" he would say, "Dae ya know where yer going?" "Aye Grampa, cheerio," I would respond, and away I went. This to me was an example of how much he cared about me and that meant a lot.

Granddad was a solid guy. You could tell he worked hard his whole life. He wore slacks, shirt, cardigan and blazer everyday. All of his cardigans and blazers had patches on the elbows and possessed his own unique smell. He would roll his own cigarettes and cup the butts in his hand as if to hide it. His fingers were brown from the nicotine and stand out most to me because I thought they looked like cooked sausages. You know that soft brown color that sausages become when you fry them up in a pan. He would joke and say don't bite them.

He would always wear a scone tweed cap whenever he went out. A few times he would take me along with him to town on a Saturday but stopped when he decided to take me to the barber with him and I freaked out on him. Little did he know, I had a phobia about getting my hair cut. It was always long and bright orange when I was young. I was often referred to as a wee lassie by people who did not know me. He wasn't too happy with me after I displayed complete madness with me screaming my head off all over a hair cut. To this day, I don't know why I was so afraid of my hair getting cut but, come to think of it, I was afraid of a lot of things.

Dogs, especially Dobermans after getting attacked by the same one twice. When my Dad confronted the guy who owned the dog all he could say is "He disnae like gingers." Case closed. My Dad had no further comments since for some reason nobody liked gingers. My Dad was a ginger, and I am sure his life was hell as well, so how could he argue.

Elevators. I have no idea why I was afraid of them. It's not like I have ever had a bad experience with one before but maybe it was the fact that all kids need something to be afraid of.

And thunder and lightning. Again, no reason to be afraid of it but it scared the heck out of me. My worst fear of all would definitely be being trapped in an elevator with a Doberman and a barber during a thunder storm.

My grandfather was named Thomas "Tommy" Macfarlane. He was born on August 28, 1904, in Glasgow. Turns out he had three brothers and one sister. He married Nellie Bone and raised two boys, Tommy my uncle and David my father. Most of his life was spent playing football (soccer) and working jobs that would support him playing football. He taught and played football in India for six years as well as spent four years playing professional in Scotland for Kilmarnock. He would whistle, daily driving my Mum crazy, and he would always say "ugh ugh aye" whenever getting up from sitting down. He also had faded out tattoos on his forearms and I could never figure out what they were. When we were at school, he would go to the bookies to bet on the horses and if he did well he would bring a couple tins of beer home with him to celebrate with. Tennent's was his beer of choice.

It's a tradition in Scotland that an ice cream van would come around the neighborhood each evening. None of the vans would sell just ice cream. You could buy bottles of soda (ginger), cigarettes, candy or tea bags, even dish soap if in a pinch. Every once in a while my father would give us change for the van but instead I would save up my change to buy things I felt I needed much more than a 5 pence mixture or a scoop of ice cream which I detested. But Dad would always buy the biggest one they carried for himself. Typical Dad. With the money I saved, I decided to buy a small tin travel chess set. Each piece had a magnet to adhere it to the board. Each night I would sit in the kitchen with my Granddad having a cup of tea and eating some toast while he taught me how to play chess. Little did I know then that this would become one of my fondest memories to look back on.

We lived in a very average neighborhood with plenty of working class families around. Football was always the choice game to play wherever and whenever the boys in the neighborhood could muster a game together. Jackets, bricks or whatever we could find would mark the goal posts carefully measuring ten paces apart. Sometimes, we would play until it got too dark to see and even if it was raining we could play for hours, but it always felt like we just started.

We all inspired to be someone we admired that played professionally. Pele, Dalglish, Sounnes or Gemmell. We were taking their place on the pitch and scoring goals for our country as if the World Cup was at stake. We would never just horse around in our minds but we would be completely entrenched in our games. Hampden Park was our place of choice every time our games escalated to an international frenzy where our sole mission was to beat the stuffing out of England and capture any beloved trophy for our Scotland.

Regional Glasgow teams didn't matter to any of us. Although some fans are fanatical about their team, whether it is Rangers, Celtic, Morton or whomever, we were all friends and it didn't really matter if you supported different teams. What did matter is that you supported Scotland.

This was our home and we were defending it with a football, unbelievable skills and some jackets marking our boundaries. Scotland, in our eyes, could not have been prouder. We all dreamed of being professionals and getting the nod from the Gaffer to strip off our warm up track suits and get in the game. Putting a few away for Scotland was the greatest feeling ever. All we ever asked for was a chance.

I played on one of the local teams called the Mallard Swifts. It was a new team formed among most of the boys who attended St. Vincent's Primary School. Our practices were held at the school gym and our game days were Saturday. We would play on the orange clay pitches around East Kilbride against other teams with much more experience, like Green Hills Villa or EKYC (East Kilbride Youth Club).

Our team was looked at by the others just how I was looked at. In complete shambles, and too young, ugly, and lean to ever be successful. I was a perfect fit, I thought.

However, we proved to be contenders. Although we never won every game, we didn't loose every game either. Sure we were made up of castaways from other teams and were thought of as a joke at first, but after our first season we were all proud to be on the squad. We all carried our black Mallard Swift bags with pride instead of hiding them from taunts and teasing.

Our coach was a great guy. Mr. Murray is how we addressed him and his assistant coaches all cared for us not just as players but as people. Our first practice was held on a free clay pitch where Mr. Murray sized each of us up. After running around like we were interviewing for the national team Mr. Murray pulled us all in. He asked, "Is there any of you lads with bruises?" We all fell quiet. Afraid if we did have bruises and admitted it to him, we would be kicked off for being unfit or medically deficient for the team. After a long unusual period of silence and he was finished looking around for anybody with an arm up he said "Well, that shows me that none of you lot are trying hard enough to win the ball." You would have thought he was handing out 20 pound notes the way everybody got excited and professed their bruises to him as though we were showing off medals for valor. Pulling down socks and pulling up shorts and spotting who had the most hideous looking bruises imaginable to gain favor with Mr. Murray.

Each Saturday morning I would get 20p for my pocket money. It would always be on the kitchen window sill and, before leaving to meet up with the rest of the team, my Granddad would give me the once over. He would be the only other person up and around with me.

I would grab 10p for my morning then spend the rest upon my successful return home, hopefully triumphant in our game.

He would see me off, checking that I had everything I needed and most of all that I wore a jacket. For some reason or another I never liked or worried about wearing a jacket. What would I need a jacket for? We are playing on a real pitch with goal posts. Isn't that what jackets are for?

The weather in Scotland is always something to never take for granted. It can change in an instant and football was played when school was in session so that meant cold, rainy and windy usually. It was so cold that at halftime Mr. Murray always made sure we had a cup of soup from the thermoses he would bring from home. Now, I am a picky eater but I always looked forward to his soups. Lentil, Scotch Broth, Cream of Chicken or whatever else we would get always tasted great and was very welcome when you are literary freezing your rear end off. No matter what kind of soup with how many amount of vegetables I would clean mine off. It was the least I could do for somebody who would take the time and care to provide such a caring gesture as to feeding us at halftime. I miss that.

Even though my Granddad played football he never really taught me anything about the game. I am sure it was only because he was in his 70s but he was always keen to know how I did when I would arrive home each Saturday afternoon. My Dad on the other hand couldn't care less. I don't even think he knew I played on a team. It took me over a year to get him to buy me boots to play with. I had to borrow old ones from friends and even played one game with boots two sizes too small for me and without laces. My feet killed me after that game and I tried my best to disguise the agony I was in.

My Dad never watched me play until I was 11. His attitude was always "get out of my way." He was a thin man in stature but had a belly that protruded from his frame as though foreign and out of place. He would eat and drink like a glutton but would prefer to drink than eat should he have to prioritize between the two. He would wear slippers around the house with his work pants and a t-shirt two sizes too small. His hair was red and curly. He would put Brylcream in it each day and comb it back the way everybody did in the 1950s with the duck tail in the back. Loose hair twisted in the front and long sideburns. He would never shave on the weekends and hated being around us kids. He smoked like a chimney and drank like a fish and totally loved himself.

When he was younger, he went to America with my Granddad to visit. My father decided to stay in America and joined the American Air Force in order to do so. Being such a man of military stature, or so he thought, handing down corporal punishment was his expertise.

He would get in your face when really angry and push you up against the wall while screaming in your face the same way you see drill sergeants do in the movies. This was how he would intimidate you. Then the belt would come unloosed. Pulled out from around his waist and either wrapped halfway around his hand or folded in half. Depending on what kind of mood he was in I guess but either way you are going to be crying before he even touched you. This he enjoyed. You could see it in his eyes. The pleasure he was about to serve himself up was noticeable in his eyes every time.

Some days I think my skin spent more time in contact with his belt than his trousers did. This was just the way it was. I don't think I ever was a really bad kid, I was just a kid. Say the wrong thing, show up late or argue with your sisters was cause enough.

Being struck by the belt was never pleasant especially when you are bullied into a corner, taking up the fetal position and being told not to defend yourself. Defending yourself was in itself cause for more punishment. It was a natural reaction to what was going on and completely unnatural not to do so I thought. It was always hard for me to not protect myself and that always caused more lashes.

By the time I was 8, his belt had become more and more flimsy either due to normal wear and tear or by how many times he used it on us. But either way it never hurt as bad as it did previously. Now I looked at this as to my advantage since it would still hurt, but it would not hurt as bad as it could have, if it had not been so worn. I never liked getting the belt, but who does? I wanted to avoid the wrath of my Dad at all costs, even if it meant lying to get out of it. But, it was always the consequence for what I thought was being disobedient by way of just being a kid. Something I think all parents struggle with, with exception of my Dad. He didn't struggle. He liked it.

In the summer of 1976, my Mum and older sister Lauren went to visit America. They were gone for two weeks visiting family in New Jersey. Upon their return my Mum had gifts for all of us. After going through the suitcases as if it is Christmas morning, each of us kids receiving our gifts from afar, satisfying our needs of something thoughtful. I received two leisure suits, baseball cap, jacket and a baseball glove. Then suddenly Mum turned to my Dad and said, "This is for you."

Well, I couldn't believe what I saw. I did know that America was the home of cowboys but had absolutely no idea until now that these cowboys could be identified with their belts. She handed him the largest, thickest strip of leather I had ever seen.

All the happiness I felt with seeing my Mum home, getting some new clothes and getting outside on a beautiful July day was drained from not just my emotions but my soul when I saw his new weapon. I never looked at it as a functional garment accessory but rather as a tool he used to inflict pain.

I knew it was only a matter of time before I would be getting better acquainted with his new belt. What hurt most was I got really mad at my mother for even considering getting him a belt. She knew what it was used for! Couldn't she get him a shirt that fit instead? Was this meant to be a warning to us that things were going to get tougher?

The sad thing was, whenever any of us got the belt, we all cried. It was never easy to watch or especially hear but this was going to get worse. Much worse.

I remember it like it was yesterday. The very next day I was the first in line to be baptized by the new belt. I was out late that day playing football at my friend Brian Duffy's house, which was on the other side of town.

Now one thing to keep in mind was I never liked being home. Even though I knew deep down I wasn't that great at football, it kept me out of the house. After moving to America, it was hard to find other kids that played soccer but I did whatever I could to stay outside.

Learned American football. Played stickball. I even joined the science club to build model rockets and shoot them off at the Gunnel Oval, a local sports complex. I did what I could to stay away from the house. Back in East Kilbride, Scotland, I kind of knew after our football game that I might be in trouble for being out late and missing dinner. But I wouldn't say I missed it. Dinner was always terrible but I'll get into that later on. I took my time getting home even though I was late. I was in no hurry but, to be honest, I did forget about the new belt. I had an "I don't care" attitude, until of course I was confronted with the consequences for disobedience.

Even in school whenever we acted up, or even behaved like the normal kids we were, we would get the belt. Sometimes, the teacher would deliver the punishment and that was tough because we all liked our teacher, Mrs. Angel. She was a very attractive lady that was always dressed to the highest standard. She had perfect blonde hair every day and we were all crazy about her. She would put on this stern prune face when delivering the belt. You would have to stand in front of her with your right arm outstretched palm to the ceiling and your left hand supporting the right. The belt was about 18 inches long with cut tares of about 6 inches on the end that would hit your hand. Although none of us would cry when receiving it, I think if we could cry in front of the whole class we would have. She was always kind enough to excuse you to the bathroom afterwards with a classmate in order to collect yourself. That gesture always showed us just how much class she really had.

Her boss, the head master, was the complete opposite. Mr. Dolan or, as we liked to call him, Smokey Dolan, because we used to see him smoking on occasion, was a giant of a man and his belt hits were unbelievably painful. With your hands outstretched he would come down with what felt like the full wrath of God. Your hands would sting for what felt like hours. The crazy thing is, whenever I got the belt in school, it meant I would get the belt at home also. Guaranteed.

After I walked in the door from coming home late that beautiful July evening my father was ready for me. It was as if he was able to see me coming down the street whistling and skipping as though I hadn't a worry in the world.

As soon as I walked in he was right there in my face. Our house had a long hallway right inside the door with the kitchen off to the immediate right and a bathroom to your immediate left. In typical Scottish fashion all rooms had doors, unlike in America were everything is open in the common areas. We had a box at the side of the front door for everyone to put their shoes in upon entering the house. You were never allowed to wear shoes in the house.

My father was hunched over in my face inquiring about my whereabouts, as if he really cared. Was he worried? That's a laugh. Arms placed behind his back and biting his bottom lip as he always did before unleashing his punishment. As he backed me up to the door I had just closed, I wished it would let me back out. But it wasn't going to. Not today. After trying to explain I was playing football with my hands in front of me to create some space and my back against the door he unleashed a pain that I had never felt before. The belt struck my left thigh so hard that at first it felt numb. I fell into the box containing all the shoes as if someone pulled me down into it. The pain was so excruciating that I could not scream or cry in pain. All I could do was inhale as if I had been drowning and fighting for my breath. I had never felt this before. I think that is why it still stands out so vividly. After finally being able to compose a yell in response to my agony and what seemed like a long time I got another whack just in case the first one didn't quite get the point across. At this point I hated everything in my life. I was in so much pain, slipping further and further into the box of shoes and curling up into a pathetic sniveling little ball that has been sunk to the lowest level possible.

Even my sisters felt sorry for me. It was bad. The welts on my leg were huge and very sensitive. I could barely walk after he told me to get up. I didn't want to get up. I wanted to just stay there in the box and figure out how I can get to bed without it hurting so bad.

Bruises? You want to see bruises Mr. Murray? I'll show you some of the best.

## BEING GINGER

My name on the football team was Ginger. No one knew me as David. This was simply because of my large, curly mop of red, more like orange, hair. This was a common name for all redheads and was always used as a derogatory term and never one of compliment. I never cared to be called Ginger but no matter how hard I tried it seemed every time I would say "my name is David," the response was always with a laugh and "Aye right son, now get playing Ginger."

Now, you would think that being a ginger in Scotland was normal and not something out of the ordinary. Wrong. You get more slagging than anyone and you're always looked at as different. I suppose I was different but surely not because of my pasty pale skin, my freckled face and arms or the combination of all of the above with thin slit eyes that earned me another nickname, China Man. It didn't help that I bought chopsticks at a school ramble sale one year and used them to eat everything. I would carry them in my sleeve and pull them out as if relishing in smuggling some contraband through customs and admiring my tools while watching David Carradine in Kung-Fu.

Two of my sisters are redheads, my Dad was a redhead, his mother was a redhead and I am sure it goes back generations as far back as the Macfarlanes and Bones line can be traced. Still, we were never fully accepted for who we are, just gingers. The picking on me would be terrible at times and I could only wish God would see it in his good graces to remove this curse and please turn my hair brown. Nae chance.

I absolutely hated how I looked as a boy. I was skinny, freckled, short and ginger. I had every strike against me and no matter how hard I worked at a normal life, these physical attributes would haunt me for years to come, all the way until I was about 21.

Gingers, I believe, are the most picked on and discriminated against people in the world. Even in Scotland, where there are a higher percent of redheads per capita than any other country. You would think that with that many redheads there would be some respect for us. But there was none whatsoever.

For anyone that has red hair, you end up taking such banter that it is sometimes hard to endure. I can't tell you how much I wished things were different but it was extremely hard being someone that I had absolutely no control over. The teasing and open disrespect is so blatant and wicked it is as if redheads are born with absolutely no feelings what so ever. You are almost never referred to by name but always "the ginger kid."

If you grew up with red hair then you know what I am talking about. If not, then you're lucky.

The weird thing is that it doesn't matter to anyone else how hard a time you could get from others. The level of teasing is beyond reproach. It's as if you're not even human sometimes. It's so bad that when you would express your feelings to someone of authority about being picked on they would laugh it off as if it is never a big deal. The level of prejudice is steep towards us and very hurtful.

After moving to the States and learning about civil rights and prejudice against Blacks, Hispanics or any immigrants for that matter, you learn that tolerance and respect are important to overcome these prejudices. There have been countless leaders for each respected group that feels unjustly judged for being different with no control over the conditions from which they are born. Unfortunately, being ginger is never taking into account for being discriminated against. Because you're ginger, other kids make fun of you. Because you're ginger, girls are too embarrassed to express feelings for you in fear of being teased themselves. Because you're ginger, everyone can have a good laugh at how you look, as if being ginger discounts for any feelings that the rest of the human race has instinctively within their very being.

Even though Sir Winston Churchill, Margaret Thatcher, President Andrew Jackson, President Calvin Coolidge and even Thomas Jefferson were all gingers, you have to imagine how much scrutiny they got not for the person they were but rather because of the color of their hair.

My Mum used to say that it was bad luck to let a redhead be the first to enter your house on New Year and she would corral us up, so as not to be the one to deliver her bad luck during the New Year celebrations. All in all, gingers could have been summed up as about as lucky as breaking a mirror, spilling salt, walking under a ladder or being the black cat to cross your path.

At school in Scotland, I was the only ginger in the class. The teasing didn't come mostly from my classmates but the older classmen. It was relentless, especially from people whom I never knew. It was almost as if walking down the street with red hair was a criminal offense and anybody could say whatever they wanted to in order to hurt your feelings without repercussion.

The good that came out of this is that it helped me develop a rather tough skin. I would always pretend that it never affected me but it did. I would laugh it off most of the time in public but at home I would be miserable because of the harsh treatment from others and wondering, if I cut it off, would the teasing stop?

Now I'm not telling you this for you to feel sorry for me, but to share the torment that a redhead could sometimes be put through. If you're a redhead and reading this, I am sure you have very similar events happen to you. I am over it now, but when I see little red headed kids I sometimes feel sorry for what they have to endure. My youngest son is a redhead and he took his fair share of teasing while growing up.

Even when I was in the Navy the teasing didn't stop. But, by then, I had pretty much heard it all and it didn't sway me from doing what I wanted to do.

# THE AMERICAN DREAM

After a few weeks living in the USA with my Uncle Tommy's family and getting somewhat acquainted with our new surroundings, it was time to move into our own place. My Uncle Tommy and his family were so beneficial for us and kept us at ease while we were transitioning to not only a new country but, most importantly, a new life. His help was paramount in my life and I am forever grateful for his sincere attitude toward helping all of us get established.

Uncle Tommy was a very typical working class Scotsman. He was very honest and caring but he never wore his heart on his sleeve. He would give you the shirt off his back but you had to ask for it. That's the way most Scotsman are. It is almost as though you need the person's permission to help and you never volunteer to help for fear of offending.

Uncle Tommy looked just like his Dad, my Granddad. He had the same happy-go-lucky attitude and worked hard his whole life. It showed in the toughness of his hands and the lines in his face. A mechanic by trade, he knew everything about anything with moving parts. His claim to fame was developing a co-extrusion machine that was state of the art for its time. Since he worked for the company that needed the machine he wasn't able to obtain any patents or even recognition for his work. I could tell this hurt him but he kept soldiering on as most blue collar skilled laborers do. No need to dwell on the past was his attitude and he had to focus on his own business.

He owned an automotive machine shop with his business partner Willie Hood. Willie was also a Scottish immigrant but the funny thing was that he was the complete opposite of Uncle Tommy. Uncle Tommy was quiet, Willie was loud. It was almost comical watching the two of them interact. Willie was the sales part of the business and Uncle Tommy was the Sherpa. Their shop was littered with old cars, one of which they sold to my Dad, and their expertise was in rebuilding engines. Both men treated me as if I was their own and I am forever in their debt for doing so.

One day, my Dad dropped me off at their shop. I could tell neither of them really cared for my Dad due to his selfish, sneaky and very untrusting reputation. I think here is when I am being kind. He was the worst excuse for a human being. Anyway, Uncle Tommy and Willie decided to have me tag along all day. I loved it. Having been in the country only a couple of weeks, it was great being with these guys. And it was like being back home in Scotland, since they both spoke Scottish as if they arrived on the same plane I came on. They were in country for about 20 years each at this time, but you would never know by how they spoke.

Even though Scottish is quite frankly English but with a brogue, Americans have a very hard time understanding the Scottish accent. Mostly because we speak fast and use a lot of slang, and, in my opinion, Americans have a very hard time listening to accents. I will elaborate later about this, so back to the Willie and Uncle Tommy show.

Their shop was on the banks of the Passaic River in Lyndhurst, New Jersey. There were mountains of snow everywhere and it was really cold out, so I spent most of my time in the garage drinking hot tea and looking around for something to do. Both Willie and Uncle

Tommy kept me well entertained. Most of the time they both made fun of my long hair. "You look like a lassie," they would joke adding a few other digs here and there, but I loved it because of the attention I was getting from these guys. After a tour of the garage and demonstrations of all the equipment, they took me to lunch. We jumped into Willie's Datsun pickup truck, which was really small by American standards, with me squeezed in the middle.

Down the road we ended up going to the Lyndhurst Diner. For anyone who isn't familiar with New Jersey, diners are an important part of life in New Jersey. This was the first time I was in a restaurant in America. I thought it was great how they had spinning dessert displays with these super tall cakes and pies. We sat at the counter and I was so impressed by the swivel over-padded seat that you would have thought I was on a carnival ride. It wasn't long before Uncle Tommy grabbed the back of my chair and focused my attention on the menu.

The menu was enormous. It would have taken me half an hour to read it but, thankfully, I had these two guys to help me decipher what was what. As I said earlier, I was a picky eater so there was no way I was going to try anything new. After several minutes and a little bit of pressure to make up my mind, I decided on a plain hamburger, chips and whatever fizzy drink I could get my hands on. No meat pies, fried fish, sausage rolls or bridies on the menu, so I was feeling like I was in for something I would hate considering I wasn't very adventurous in the food arena. The meal, for the most part, wasn't memorable, with the exception of the coleslaw that came with my hamburger. Oh, and by the way, when I said plain I meant very plain.

Hamburger patty, fully cooked, on a plain bun. That's it. This is how I would eat my burgers for the next year and a half before risking eating the food of this new country.

The coleslaw was in a small, round, paper-molded ramekin filled high with finely shredded cabbage and carrots in a creamy, white, sour sauce. I had never before tasted such a food, nor thought I would enjoy it, but I loved it. I don't think that I had ever had raw cabbage before, just overcooked cabbage or overcooked brussel sprouts which were not very good but rather memorably bad. As you already know, our food at home was pretty bad hence the reason I was always so hesitant to try something new or different. I was so impressed by the taste of the coleslaw that I asked for both Uncle Tommy's and Willie's. They happily obliged.

After lunch they took me to a barber for my first haircut in a barber shop since the ill-fated day when my Granddad had taken me and I freaked out on him. My Mum cut my hair every time after that incident and I tried to keep it long simply because I hated getting it cut. Besides it was the 70s and long hair was all the trend so it wasn't unusual to see guys with long hair. The barber they took me to was a traditional men's barber shop with the ancient swivel chair that reminded me of the Sweeny Todd story. You know, the one where you sit down for a shave, he kills you, and then dumps your body in a secret compartment beneath the floor.

After everyone had a good laugh at my long curly locks, I was instructed to take my place in a booster seat on the barbers chair and face my fears. I pretended not to be bothered but I was petrified. Clean back and sides where the instructions and all I could do is watch my hair falling on the apron in huge clumps while the electric clippers were tearing huge chunks from my skull, or at least that's what it felt like. After the haircut, I felt as if my head was naked. Lighter and colder but very embarrassed at how I looked in the mirror. It wasn't me. I wasn't mad but disappointed. I know they meant well and I'm pretty sure I did need it cut but this was extremely short. From one extreme to another, I was transformed into what they thought a ten-year-old boy should look like.

To top it all off, it was much colder in New Jersey than what it was in Scotland. I didn't have a winter coat to combat the elements of my new surroundings and now my ears were freezing. So Willie and Uncle Tommy took me to a clothing store where they bought me a denim Levi jacket with wool lining inside and on the collar. This jacket was the second nicest one I ever wore. My first being an expedition-style army coat with a fur trimmed hood that I just loved. It was olive drab green with a zipper and snaps and I thought it was the best jacket that I ever had. Ready for any expedition life was willing to deal. I can still smell that jacket to this day. It was great. The denim jacket came in a close second.

After being fed, cut and covered, we headed back to the garage where I made us all tea. It was a great day and quite honestly the best day I had in America so far and for some time to come. I felt special that day, especially because I was getting attention and the fact that I was around the guys for the first time in my life.

Although I spent quite a bit of time with my Granddad we only spent that time at home and my sisters were always there. For anyone growing up with sisters you know they demand a large amount of attention. I don't believe they did so on purpose; it's just the way it was I guess. So there was very little opportunity to spend time with the men. And my Dad wasn't the guy to teach me how to behave when I was older. His philosophy was children should be rarely seen and never heard. To put it bluntly, he just didn't care enough, but my feelings were never hurt because I just didn't know any better.

But I truly loved this day.

I got over the haircut by the time we were back at the garage. I wandered around outside for a few minutes checking out the old cars in the lot and jumping off the snow mounds after we had our tea. In the garage's office, which was cluttered with dirt-coated parts books, invoices and a water cooler that dispersed the hot water for the tea, was a sign above one of the two desks which read,

"In God we trust, All others cash!"

I thought that was the funniest thing I ever read. And coming from somebody who read "Oor Wullie," one of the most popular Scottish cartoons in the world, on a regular basis, that is quite impressive.

"Do you know what that means?" Willie asked.

"Aye, you don't trust anybody?" I said.

"If you canny (can't) afford it, you canny get it," Willie said.

I thought about it for a second but didn't really get what he was saying. I could tell by his expression he knew I was thick.

"It means you don't accept credit. You follow me?" Willie said after what seemed like a long pause. Willie went on to tell me how the credit system works and how it works against you. He went on to tell me how it is best to avoid debt as much as possible. Summing it all up while singing the lyrics to the old Tennessee Ford song "Sixteen Tons."

"Sixteen tons and what do you get? Another day older and deeper in debt."

Later in life, following Willie's advice, I came across a book of genius written by another Scotsman named "An Inquiry into the Nature and Causes of the Wealth of Nations" by Adam Smith. When I reflect on that book, I think of Willie's advice and that's how you can pretty much sum it up.

"Sixteen tons and what do you get? Another day older and deeper in debt."

If you listen to the words of that song, which I highly recommend, it's like a history lesson all in itself.

Years later, when I went to work for Willie, I would see that sign and it always reminded me of that special day.

Willie went on to tell me all the makes of cars they were working on and of course quizzed me on what I was learning in school. He was a very intelligent man and liked to let you know he was. Willie was far from humble and, the funny thing was, Uncle Tommy was completely humble.

"Have you learned logarithms yet?" Willie asked.

"No," I replied with a confused look on my face, having absolutely no idea what he was talking about.

"Mathematics, what do you know about mathematics?" he said very loudly as if he was talking over me to get someone else's attention.

"Ugh, leave him alone," Uncle Tommy said, shaking his head as if in disapproval.

Willie continued with, "You need to know everything about mathematics. It's the most important lesson you'll ever need to know. You don't want to grow up stupid do you?"

Logarithms were a discovery of John Napier, a 17th century mathematician who was also from Scotland. They were used to simplify calculations quickly. I never learned about logarithms in high school formally, but I applied some time to learn them on my own. Thanks to Willie.

"No," was all I could say. I felt really stupid all of a sudden since I had no idea where he was going with this.

Willie gave me more advice that day than I have ever gotten in my life and I stuck to everything he said as if God himself was commanding me. Willie was a tough guy. Short and stout with hands like a vice and a loud screechy laugh. I could tell he was very serious though in his questioning what I know. I think he was sizing me up to see what I was made of. I didn't mind though because I was really enjoying the day. It was a beautiful, clear sky, sunny day even though it was colder than I had ever experienced before and I always look back on that day as the best I ever had as a kid.

"What do you know about Scotland?" Willie asked.

"I don't know," was my reply and I am sure you know by now what a mistake that was. I wish I could have thought of a better answer than that but I was feeling very intimidated by now. I was expecting him to lose his temper and I would end up looking as in despair as the cars needing fixing in the lot.

Willie just shook his head in disbelief. To be honest with you, I was relieved not to get the verbal lashing that I had coming to me.

"Where are you from?" he asked sarcastically. Now sarcasm I was very accustomed to since my Dad wrote the book.

"Scotland," I said in confidence.

"Are you sure?" he continued. "Because you don't know anything about it."

"Aye," I said, feeling the split second of confidence I had a millisecond ago fade rather quickly.

"What do you know about it," Willie said, in a slow loud voice as if I was hard of hearing as well as not fully understanding the question. He must have thought I was thick or something. I wish I had the capacity to handle myself better but it would take me years to do so.

"I don't know, the normal stuff they teach you in school, I guess," I said as if dismissing his questioning as though telling him he shouldn't be so serious when I'm supposed to be having fun. Man, did I feel stupid.

Willie went on to tell me his version of Scotland the exact same way as most Scotsman talk about when bragging about their home and rightfully so. It's almost impossible to have a conversation with a Scotsman without Scottish inventions being brought up.

"Scotland has way more contributions to our civilized world than any other people," usually leads the conversation. Then we go into the inventions, the statesmen, the heritage of innovation and most importantly Scottish ingenuity.

When you listen and understand how great Scottish accomplishments are it really makes you quite proud of Scotland. A side of the country that isn't involved in fighting the English, which seems to be the assumption of most Scots from foreigners, or just fighting in general. The rough, tough, kilt-wearing highlander, slaying enemies by the thousands is usually the romantic side of Scotland capitalized on by the likes of Sir Walter Scott and made into film, portraying the barbaric life north of the border as anything but intelligent.

The point Willie was getting at, of course I did not get it at the moment, was you need to learn on your own. Don't just take what you're told to learn but rather learn on your own. It took me three years to learn that lesson. Once learned, I applied this to my own education. Reading what I wanted to read and doing what I wanted to do to further myself was a lesson for the life I have lived, with thanks to Willie. The impression he left with me has affected me forever. And I mean that in the most positive way.

I didn't want that day to end but it did. It wasn't long before my Uncle Tommy got me into the Country Squire station wagon and we headed off to his house for me to join up with my family in order to pack up and head to an apartment my Dad rented for us to live in until he closed on the house he was buying.

I rode with Uncle Tommy and two of my sisters to the apartment. It was only about a twenty minute drive from his house into the next town of Kearny.

"What a dump," was what I thought. We entered up some stairs that were creaking as if about to give in, and stepped into our apartment, which was on the main avenue above a pizzeria.

I wondered what we were doing here. All I could think of was how disgusting and appalling these conditions were and how much I missed home. There was a front room, a kitchen, a bathroom and two bedrooms. Did I mention the place was a dump?

It made our house in Scotland look like a palace. I was so ashamed of living here that I purposely gave my parents a hard time for making us live in such a dump. The front room was where my parents slept with Carole our youngest sister. The rest of us shared the two back bedrooms, with two beds in each really small room.

There were cockroaches everywhere and I was freaking out since I had never seen these bugs before in my life. Our old house never had bugs.

There was a bright plastic pizza sign just outside the front window and it would light up the front room so bright at night my Dad would complain all the time about it. The smell was nauseating as if the odor was permanently embedded into the cheap paint covering the twenty layers of paint beneath it. Every time you would turn on the bathroom light or open a cabinet in the kitchen, cockroaches would scurry everywhere and I just couldn't cope with it. Even now, thinking back, I get such a creepy feeling about that apartment.

My feelings toward the apartment pretty much summed up how I was feeling about the whole situation with the move and the area we were in. I was miserable and probably miserable to be around. I really missed home and couldn't think of any reason my parents would want to stay here. Even from watching American television shows while in Scotland, I wasn't impressed and this experience was holding true to my expectations.

The owners of the pizza restaurant we lived above complained constantly about the noise we were producing upstairs. What else do you expect with five kids running around and nowhere to play outside? I was going mad as I am sure my sisters were also.

It wasn't long before we were moving into an actual house and I couldn't wait. I am sure the pizza restaurant owners were just as happy as I was. My parents got a house about five blocks east of the apartment, off the main avenue, on Forest Street. Although it was better than the apartment, it was a really old house and needed a ton of work. And work that my Dad would start but never finish, except for hiring renovators to replace the outdated aluminum kitchen cabinets with wooden cabinets and updated counters. Needless to say, I was still unhappy.

After we settled into the house I was doing my best to be positive in trying to be happy. I didn't have any friends and really didn't know my way around, so I found it hard to be stuck in the house. I missed, more than anything, playing football. After starting school, I was only focused on trying to get on a team but it turned out that school didn't have a sports program until high school so I had to go find a team somehow.

I pestered my Dad to take me to the football fields at a park called the Gunnel Oval. It was a sports park with baseball fields and football (soccer) pitches. It turned out that we ran into a team practicing, with kids around my age, and my Dad talked to the coach.

He was happy to have me on board and I was happy to be on board. This would also be the first time I would play on a grass pitch. Back home it was only orange gravel that we played on that would hurt really bad if you fell.

Finally, I was doing what I loved to do best.

# HOMESICK

Starting school in America made me miss home the most. The kids were different. Loud, obnoxious at times, well most times, with terrible eating habits in the lunch room. So, I would opt to walk home everyday for lunch just to avoid the ill-mannered display going on in the lunch room. Besides, I wasn't a fan of the food and my parents weren't the type to pack a lunch. They gave us one dollar between the four of us, Carole was in daycare, and all we could afford was four bags of Wise Potato Chips at twenty five cents each. One day, I was so sick from lack of eating I ended up in the nurse's room where she fed me some crackers and told me how important it is to eat. I didn't dare tell her all I ate was potato chips each day but I was embarrassed by the situation I was in.

In Scotland, we got a hot meal everyday, on a real plate, with a dessert after. We used silverware and were instructed on how to use them properly. Fork in left hand, with the arch facing up, knife firmly in right hand and used to push the food onto the fork. With the arch upward you would be prevented from overloading the fork as you would do if inverted to shovel the food in. Small portions at a time so your mouth was never stuffed. Placing the fork at the piece of food you were eating and cutting around it made ease of eating rather than stabbing, cutting, putting the knife down and switching hands to eat.

We would usually have mince (ground beef) and tatties (potatoes) but on occasion we would have curry and rice. I can still smell the curry. It was divine. I would practically lick the plate. Usually it consisted of a Tika Masala of chicken or lamb. Man, was

43

that stuff ever good. At home, my Dad did most of the cooking and it usually always involved deep fat frying. We could never get him to make curry in the house because my Mum would never allow the smell in her house. She would say, "It lingers for days." Fish sticks and chips were normally what we got as a treat but we would have boiled fish or stovies some of the time.

Stovies, to this day, is my all time favorite meal. Peeled and cut potatoes, boiled with minced beef, onions and carrots, and seasoned with Bovril, a concentrate of beef very much like a glace (reduction pronounced glass) invented by a Scottish butcher named John Lawson Johnston. Johnston was also a keen student of food science and perfected concentrating beef and preserving it for a long shelf life so well he was later contracted to supply the beef for the French Army during the Franco-Prussian War. For his efforts, he was awarded the Order of the French Red Cross. Not bad for a butcher from Edinburgh.

Stovies without the Bovril, in my opinion, was somehow missing the pizzazz that made it so special. If you had no Bovril then scratch making the stovies for there is no suitable substitute. My Mum, who was usually a terrible cook, had a knack for making stovies and her stovies were the best. Perfect every time. On especially poor days, she would put a slice of bread underneath our portions to bump up the portion so it would fill us up with less of all the other ingredients. Every culture has its peasant food I guess and stovies would be ours. I would hope even The Queen would have tried stovies, because if she hadn't it would be a terrible loss.

The weather started getting warm, really warm. This was nice at first but before long I was feeling sick from the heat. I couldn't wait for school to finish. The heat was unbearable as were the kids in class.

That summer, I met a few kids in the neighborhood. This was great since it gave me an excuse to keep out of the house. They were fascinated with how funny I spoke and how hard it was to understand me especially since that I was speaking English. In school I also had a hard time communicating. I was placed in a remedial class to work on my pronunciation. Basically, English as a second language. They were probably trying to ensure that I wouldn't have an issue with my lessons since we were studying the Revolutionary War and needed to make sure I knew how the Americans beat the British forces to gain independence. I couldn't care less but nobody had a problem letting me know the British lost.

I missed Scotland more than anything. I missed the smell of the air, the grass, the rain and most of all I missed my Granddad. The World Cup was going on and I missed the historic Scotland vs. Holland game on June 11th. I was sure everybody back home was going absolutely nuts watching the game and all us kids would be wearing the beloved Umbro Scotland kit trying to imitate Archie Gemmill dodging defenders to score a win for Scotland. Man, the place must have been amazing and I was missing out.

Granddad would have placed a bet on the World Cup at the bookies. He loved to play the horses and did so religiously. Paper in jacket pocket, cap on and off to the bookie with a circle around which race and horse to bet on. On a good day when he would come home with his cans of Tennent's Lager, he would whistle while moving from room to room. "Pure magic," he would say.

After we moved, he went to live with his sister and died on the 4th of July, 1978. When everyone around me was lighting off fireworks, I couldn't help but feel terrible for my Granddad. We would never enjoy our tea together again. We would never have our nightly chess matches and, worst of all, I would never have that male role model to look up to ever again. I certainly wasn't going to get it from my Dad. We didn't even like each other. Later on, I would make an attempt but all that did was reconfirm that he was more interested in himself.

Summers in Scotland are special to me. Although it wouldn't get as warm as America it was still pleasant. Never humid. It would stay light until around eleven o'clock at night and the air was always clean feeling. The midgies would be about the only pests but as a kid they were never a bother. The grass would be the greenest grass you'd ever seen.

My school back in Scotland would host a two-week summer session where you could take art classes, play sports, socialize and watch pantomimes and puppet shows for five pence. We thought it was great going to school in clothes other than our school uniforms and blazers. There was table tennis, net ball and tons of fun for everybody. Everybody had a great time.

Although a lot of my friends would take trips with their families in the summer to Inverness, Loch Lomond or Edinburgh, our parents didn't take us anywhere. Well, one time they took us to Largs in the winter during what seemed like a blooming hurricane. The waves were crashing over the sea wall and we couldn't get out of the car. It was terrible.

A few times I got the chance to escape with my friends on day trips. Whenever asked, I never hesitated to rush home and beg my parents for permission and play the game of "Ask your Dad", "Ask your Mum." If only they could be in the same room for Pete's sake.

I love the scenery when driving around Scotland. Seeing the castles, winding narrow roads and stone walls. The hills and mountains are beautiful to see and sometimes dark and eerie. The water from field streams is delicious and freezing cold. The water in Scotland has its own taste that's hard to describe. Really clean and refreshing. Actually delicious to drink unlike the tap water in New Jersey which was so heavily chlorinated that it was cloudy.

Scotland's fields were always fun to walk through in the summer, as was hanging out in the woods making swings out of whatever we could find tied to a stick to sit on. The days seemed to go on forever and we loved venturing out, having a picnic, sharing a bottle of Irn Bru, and enjoying crackers and cheese or yogurt and fruit. We always had a football at our feet and plenty of places to play.

There was a set of garages behind our house back in Scotland and a small strip of grass where we would have most evening games. There was a sign over the garages prohibiting ball games but as long you stayed on the grass and didn't dent any cars or garage doors nobody minded. Every once in a while a few of the neighborhood dads would come out and kick the ball around with us. That was always great fun. It could be two against five of us and they would clean our clocks but we knew they were too tired to be running around past a half hour with us so we would laugh at the old winded geezers when they couldn't take any more.

Our neighborhood was mostly made up of working class families that weren't interested in competing with each other. The focus was to just keep working. There were no unemployed around us thanks to the proximity of the industrial parks and everybody's needs were met.

My Mum worked as a seamstress in a tartan factory making kilts and made some extra money making kilts and other clothes at home. My Dad, well I never really kept track of what he was doing other than engineering school some evenings and different day jobs that I lost track of. One year, he worked as a delivery man for a shipping company. That was the best Christmas we ever had in our lives. Every one of our presents were thanks to his ability to steal everything he sees and left, I'm sure, a lot of unhappy children around Renfrewshire due to their presents not showing up.

At the time I never really thought of us as being poor but we were struggling to get by. Scotland is not an easy place to be financially successful due to most jobs being hard labor jobs in a very competitive market with limited growth and low wages. Unlike how it is in America where most wealth is based on debt, nobody in our neighborhood had a house any different than the rest of us and nobody at the time owned nor mortgaged the house they lived in. The Council owned the house and you paid a rent commensurate to your income. We lived on the end house in a row of four, surrounded by similar homes. No-one stood out above the other, other than how clean your windows were or how nice of curtains you had hanging.

48

If my friends and I had a few pence we would catch the bus to the town center. Hopefully catching the double-decker, where we would go upstairs and try to bag the front seat beholding the best view. If we didn't have enough for both the bus fare and chips in town we opted to walk, saving our money for the chips. Seemed like forever to get there on foot but when you're eight or nine years old it's just another adventure and it seemed as though we had all the time in the world. We would graze through the shopping center, looking and touching everything we could get away with, while making mental notes for our Christmas lists. The annual Scotland football uniform was at the top of everybody's list. Mine especially. I only got it once and that was Christmas of 1977. The best present I ever got in my opinion.

We would go to the Olympia Disco which was a dancing hall in town and check out the lassies. None of us ever had the courage to talk to any of them but it was always fun. The music would be bumping with all the latest hits blaring away. It was ten pence to get in on a Saturday afternoon and the place would be packed full of kids running around and dancing like monkeys freshly sprung from the zoo. Good times. Guaranteed you were walking home after a visit to the Olympia since whatever money you had left over went to a bottle of Irn Bru and some crisps or chips if you had enough money.

The winters in Scotland were often rainy, dark and cold but nowhere near as cold as it gets in America. It would seem as though the sun would skip over us some days and we would be stuck in a perpetual state of darkness. Go to school in the dark. Go home from school in the dark. We would get playtime breaks in school which were great. One in the morning and one in the afternoon. That's the only time you would get a hint of daylight since every class I sat in each year had the desks turned with our backs to the window to keep us from daydreaming and focused on the black boards. Suffering through the winter made the summer all the more worth while.

But now, I was in America. And I was homesick for Scotland. I know being homesick could sometimes make you depressed but I didn't let it get to me that bad. I really did try to make the best of my situation. The new environment was also a big change for our family. My Dad became more distant. While my Mum was doing her best, I could see how the change was also affecting her, especially managing five kids.

My Dad started turning into a real jerk, more and more as the year came to a close. Our house had a den in the downstairs behind the kitchen and this became my room to share with the dog. I was the one responsible for taking care of her and letting her in and out. She was a terrier coyote mix of some sort but a good dog to have around. And every morning, my bed was kicked and my Dad would encourage me to take the dog out with a profanity enhanced command. It was lovely to wake up to "Boy, get up and get the ------- dog out." I hated and dreaded what turned out to be an every morning ritual.

Just outside my back door was a small porch where I kept the chain for the dog and also where I staged the trash bags before leaving in the morning to put them in the can on my way to school. Toward Christmas, my Mum bought my Dad a quarter keg of beer which he put in the back porch to keep it cold since we didn't have a fridge big enough to hold it. I knew my Dad liked to drink but it wasn't until this point that I had any idea he was a raging alcoholic. And when I say raging, I am not exaggerating.

He was constantly going back to fill up his mug with beer. Now, being Scottish, by the age of seven I had already tried beer. I didn't care for it at first but began to like it as something I would enjoy on occasion whenever it was available. It is not considered taboo in Scotland as it is in America, so at home it was always available and never frowned on for trying, just as long you didn't steal it. You had to ask permission.

One night, I didn't ask permission when it came to getting some beer from the keg. It was late, and nobody was downstairs, so I decided to grab a coffee cup and help myself. It wasn't bad but I enjoyed the ability to help myself without anybody around. After about the third cup I started pouring some in the dogs dish because I felt sorry for her and thought she deserved some beer just as much as I did. I didn't have any problem sleeping that night on the couch that I slept on, with my blue Star Wars sheets, and neither did the dog.

But the next morning it wasn't just a kick that woke me up. It was my Dad, grabbing me by the hair and neck, pulling me out of bed, screaming. Apparently, the beer didn't agree with the dog's digestive system and she had diarrhea. He had no idea we were drinking his beer that night but had every intention in the world to show me the mess and making me clean it up. He went ballistic. He was shoving me right down in it and the dog was cowering in another side of the room only to be kicked by him after he was done kicking me to get it cleaned up.

I never did that again, but I was so sore at him. All I could think of was how I could poison his beer to make him sick. I hated

51

him. It was hard enough dealing with the crap of moving to another country but now I was really starting to feel absolute hatred for him no matter how hard he tried to make it up to me. Well, actually, he never tried to make it up to me which was no surprise. It was hard enough to get him to buy me two dollar football boots from a discount store so I could play football when he was in a good mood, so I don't know why I would think he owed me. He never owed me anything in his eyes and he wasn't afraid to let me know it either.

So from this point on, I tried to find every excuse to stay out of the house. I joined the Civil Air Patrol for flying lessons and to take evening classes. I joined the Space and Astronomy Club. I played intramural sports in the morning before school and whatever I could find after school. It was only when my parents demanded I come home after school to do my chores around the house that I forced myself back to the house.

Ever since I can remember, we all did duties around the house. My parents were big coffee and tea drinkers but they never made it themselves. We made it. It was our job to put the kettle on, make the drinks and serve them. They got up for nothing.

I always got stuck doing dishes or other jobs around the house that were hard for my sister to do like pulling weeds and cutting the grass. I hated it but didn't know any better. I didn't want the belt and I did my best to avoid confrontation as much as possible. We had to go to the shops for cigarettes or milk or whatever else they needed. Back then kids could buy cigarettes just as long you had the money.

One evening, we were sitting in the living room watching the telly and I was having a terrible day. My Dad was giving me a real hard time working around the house and I was in no mood for talking. My older sister Lauren asked me if I wanted to sign her yearbook since she was moving from middle school to high school. I told her I couldn't sign it because I didn't know how to spell Kunta Kinte. Whack, I got it right across the jaw as if my Dad was power hitting Mohammed Ali to gain the title in a prize fight.

I saw stars and then I got the belt across my thigh. I am sure he was biting his lower lip as he usually does but I couldn't see and for the first time in a long time I didn't really feel the belt since my face and ear was killing me. I felt like I was going to puke and my eyes swelled up with tears. My sisters were all crying and my Dad was yelling at everybody to shut up.

All I could think about for days after this happened was that I just wanted to go home to Scotland. I missed my home more than anything. I missed the comfort of everything familiar. I thought I missed it before but now I felt like I was in exile with an uncontrollable power keeping me from what I previously took for granted. I was sorry for this situation and saw no way out of it. If I could have swam three thousand miles home I would have.

Over the next few months things became more and more unbearable. My Dad took a job in Miami and left us. All of us. Each day my emotions were mixed, having both joy and sadness fill my heart.

After about four weeks my Dad came back to New Jersey but wasn't living with us. He was renting a single room in some dive apartment house on the outskirts of town on the Kearny-Harrison border. My Mum ended up selling the house. Of course at the time we had no idea she couldn't afford it and we ended up moving into another dump apartment on the opposite side of town. Again, all I wanted was to go home to Scotland.

At this point my parents were officially separated, with divorce proceedings to follow.

My Mum gave us a choice on who to live with.

# GOODBYE TO NORMALCY ·

After my parents split up, my Mum and us kids moved to our small apartment while I started trying to regain a relationship with my Dad. I don't know why, but I felt I needed to give it a try. Put the past behind me and give him a chance to correct his wrongs by starting over with a new attitude. He knew I liked to build model airplanes so he started buying me ones that he would never buy for me before and I was taken in by this. "Maybe he does want to have a relationship with me," I thought.

I would visit with him, whenever I could, once a week. He would openly drink whisky in front of me, something that he never did previously, and I didn't like it. He talked about traveling across the US, asking if I wanted to join him. Of course I did. I would do anything to get out of Kearny. Little did I know, he was drunk at the time and just talking nonsense.

After a few months of these visits, my Mum told me that if I wanted to spend time with him then I should move out permanently to be with him full time. Now, I didn't know at the time that he was not sending my Mum any money to support us and she was really struggling financially taking care of all five kids on her own. Under the stress, she certainly was no joy to be around.

So I packed up my stuff and moved in to be with my Dad full time. He was a mess. Drinking and getting drunk every night and working for some fork lift company in the industrial section of Kearny. He lost all his cars and was taking the bus to work. My Mum drove some old AMC Pacer. She ended up getting a higher-paying seamstress job in Paramus, NJ, at the Playtex Bra Company.

Life was looking pretty bad for all of us. I really admired my Mum's ability to keep her head up and soldier on despite the unfortunate circumstances we were surrounded by. She was incredibly mad at me, I found out later, for moving in with my Dad but I thought it was what she wanted. Besides, living in a house with all women was driving me crazy, all the while my Dad was promising me the world. I had no idea that it was the booze talking.

To be honest, I didn't know which way was up. I was emotionally spent and felt as if the world was ending. I had nothing to live for, I thought, and the living conditions were far from my idea of a better life.

My Dad always loved himself. He came before anybody else in his mind and didn't have a compassionate bone in his body. He would lecture me on how I needed to grow up and go to lawyer school in order to make a ton of money by beating the system somehow. He would instruct me to make sure I got my share saying, "That the world only rewards those who take what they want rather than those who wait for it."

I had no idea, half the time, what he was talking about. I didn't know what I was going to do when I grew up. All I wanted was to go home and be nothing like him. I dreaded turning out like him. I fought against any similarities we would have.

He would carouse around the local bar scene on the weekends dressed as if he owned half the town and renting a car to get around. He would Brylcreem his hear, and wear a camel hair overcoat, dress shirt, tie and suit with a fifth of whisky in his inside jacket pocket. At first, there were a few occasions where he would leave me alone for the weekend. Eventually, this became the norm.

I didn't have money for food or anything else for that matter. All I had was the money I was saving for a trip I was going on in April of 1981 to watch the first space shuttle launch. I had joined the Aerospace club, as they were all going to witness this historic event.

At this point in my life I became very academic outside of school. I hated school more than anything in America and focused all my energy on learning as much as I could on my own. I studied aerospace science, flight training, engineering, the history of World War I and II, political science and, most importantly, law just in case Dad was on to something.

I read as many books as I could handle without making the other kids think I was a book worm. I spent countless days in the library and book stores just to cure my desire to learn. Reading was my escape. I would read very little fiction but the few fiction books that I did read I enjoyed because they helped me think of something else other than this crappy life I was living.

I hated the fact that all of our lives are governed by law, yet school never taught us anything about law. You would think that it would be just as important as math or English in order to excel in life, be a positive influence in society and know your rights. Somehow that's not the case, yet we are told ignorance is no excuse for breaking the law, so I took it upon myself to study the law. Every Sunday evening, I would watch a show called The Paper Chase on PBS about law students enduring the wrath of a tough law professor at Harvard. I had no desire to go to Harvard; I just enjoyed some of the law references within the show and never really cared for the drama side of it.

I loved thumbing through dictionaries. Black's Law Dictionary was my favorite as well as the huge Webster's Dictionary that sat upon its own podium in the library. I also took it upon myself to study the works of Robert Louis Stevenson. A man I could truly relate to since he was known to have trouble fitting in as a child and I felt that way ever since we moved to America. He liked his hair long, as did I, and he was very unconventional. A true artist. I would later visit Saranac Lake in New York and reflect upon his being there as well as in Hawaii. He was a brilliant man that I admired ever since reading "Kidnapped" when I was going to school in Scotland. "Treasure Island" was my favorite work from him and I was extremely impressed by the dark side of the "Strange Case of Dr. Jekyll and Mr. Hyde." A fascinating study of human abilities, I thought, where a drug could separate good and evil. This idea made me think of my Dad, with whisky being the drug.

Sir Walter Scott, Robert Burns, David Hume and Adam Smith were the authors of works I marveled in while trying to understand life and purpose. It would take me hours, repeatedly reading passages and trying to make sense of what I was reading and leaving it up to my own interpretation. That got me thinking that maybe that's what teachers are really there for, just to interpret for you and I thought, "What do I need them for?" It's not like I was learning anything in school at this point anyway. So, I kept on reading without the teachers.

I then turned my attention to the books of Moses in the Bible. The King James Version took more than two attempts, but I loved it. To this day, I still talk about what I learned and how those books led me to read the New Testament and the Old Testament, as well as the Dead Sea Scrolls. I started getting into philosophy and scientific theory.

I was puzzled as to why we weren't learning about any of these books or authors in school. Actually puzzled was an understatement. I was angry.

The more I read, the more dissatisfied I became with school. It wasn't only the education I disliked it, or lack thereof, it was also the social side of being around people that I became more and more intolerable of. I didn't have new clothes every semester. I didn't have clean cut hair and most of all I didn't have money for a social life. I couldn't afford meeting at pizza restaurants or movies, never mind asking girls on dates. What little money I did have I was saving to go to the Kennedy Space Center and there was no way I was going to miss out on this trip.

Ever since I can remember I was fascinated by flight and, most of all, space flight. One year for my birthday, I begged and begged for a model of a Saturn rocket. I thought for sure I was getting that rocket and ran home from school that day thinking of how great it was going to be to build my own Saturn rocket, only to find absolutely nothing there waiting for me. It was as if I didn't even exist. I was overcome by rage and disappointment. I threw such a fit, and my Mum had to walk me to the corner store where I ended up with a pack of candy and a cheap football.

On one weekend, my Dad told me he was going to go to Atlantic City with his new girlfriend whom he was seeing on a regular basis. I was going to stay at a friend's house that Friday night. We were camping out in his back yard in a tent since we scored some beer and had to hide it from his parents. The next day I walked back to our apartment with a wicked hangover. It was a really hot day and I had a forty minute walk ahead of me. I was looking forward to showering, getting some much needed sleep and finishing a book that I picked up at a used book store for a quarter called "The Catcher in the Rye" by J.D. Salinger. I had no idea at the time how famous the book was until I was late for a book report that next year and had to think of something fast so I did it on "The Catcher in the Rye." I wasn't going to do it in front of a class on the four books of Moses. I got enough ridicule just from having a large red mop of hair never mind delivering a sermon for a book report. After my report, the teacher went on to tell the class how great the book was and how they would enjoy reading it. I got lucky on that one.

When I got to the apartment it was peaceful. I laid down and fell asleep only to wake up to the sound of a lawn mower that sounded as if it was right next to me probably because of the hangover I was suffering from and the forty minute walk that turned out to be over an hour. I was too sick to eat and just laid in bed trying to not let the noise of the lawn mower get to me.

The next day I woke up starving. I went into the kitchen and there was absolutely nothing to eat. I didn't know what I was going to do. I also had to do laundry but didn't have any money to go to the launderette to wash clothes for school. It was Sunday, so I figured my

Dad would be home by dinner time and then I could eat and do my laundry.

Dad never showed up. By now I was really hungry, and I tried my best to think of something else other than food. I just kept reading into the night. The next day, I didn't go to school for lack of food and clean clothes and figured when my Dad made it home he would sort me out. Around dinner time that evening I couldn't take it any more. I had my money that I was saving for the trip to Florida and thought, "Well this is an emergency and I will ask my Dad for the twenty dollars I will use since it was for food and clothes." I had three bookshelves full of books and kept my money in the binding of a hard covered Encyclopedia Britannica.

After opening the book, I couldn't find the money. Two hundred and eighty dollars had vanished. I went into panic mode! I looked through every book one by one. I felt my heart racing inside. "Had I moved it?" I thought. "No, it's got to be in here somewhere." I searched all over and found no money. I was gutted. At first I thought I had lost it, and then I finally came to terms with the understanding that my Dad had stolen it. I was sick to my stomach. How could he? He knew how important this was to me, how important it was not to steal from your own family.

I cried my eyes out that night. I will never forget how that felt. I was starting to realize the type of person he really was but denied all the signs in front of me. By now I needed to eat. I was faint, feeling weak and drinking water was no longer cutting it for me. But I didn't know what to do. It wasn't until Thursday that I got a visit from my older sister Lauren. She just stopped in randomly to check on me and when I told her what had happened she went straight to the store and got me a sandwich to eat. If it wasn't for her who knows what would have happened to me.

My Dad didn't show up until that Sunday. A week after he was supposed to be back. I couldn't believe it when his attitude was, "What are you doing here?"

The first thing I did was ask about my money and if he had taken it. At first he denied it. Then he said, "Get ready, I have to take you somewhere." I went on to tell him how hungry I was and how he left me no food, no money and no way to wash my clothes. How I missed school for the whole week and was in danger of missing school the next day as well. He acted as if I wasn't even talking. He just ignored me and told me to get ready.

He pushed me in the car and drove me to my Uncle Tommy's house. "What are we doing here?" I asked. He wouldn't answer.

He begged for his brother to take me. I didn't know what was going on. I was speechless. My Uncle Tommy told him no and that he needed to take responsibility for his own family.

Years later, my Uncle Tommy had a conversation with me about this. I never had hurt feelings toward my uncle because of his decision not to take me. It wasn't his responsibility to care for me and I felt bad for him being put in this situation. He told me over and over how it wasn't that he didn't want me. I almost cried because I could see that this was hard for him to do. I reassured him I wasn't upset about it and that my Dad had no right to do that to him.

My Dad went on to take me to my Mum's apartment. I didn't know what was going on. He wouldn't talk to me. I thought it was something I did to make him angry only to realize years later that he was now with a companion and he no longer had use for me. What a fool I was. Thinking I could have a Dad was a dream, only to become a nightmare. For a long time after that I wondered why I couldn't have a Dad. What did I do in this or a previous life to be treated like this? Although I never had love in my life from a family, that still doesn't mean I didn't want a family.

Being back with my Mum was a humbling experience at first. She made it known that I had no right choosing him over her and I was embarrassed by my actions to make her think so. For me it wasn't one over the other, it was trying to become a whole person. She made me feel out of place but all I wanted to do was eat. I was starving.

I sat in the kitchen by myself and ate sliced cheddar cheese on fluffy white bread and drank instant iced tea. I still enjoy sliced cheddar on bread today because it keeps my memory of that day fresh. It was a day most would want to forget but I remember it as the day I truly lost my Dad forever.

I would only talk to him one more time after that day.

I was walking down the street and he was getting into his car at his new wife's house. I decided to approach him and ask about the money he stole from me. You see, the fact that he stole it still bothered me and to be honest I had a hard time with his decision to take it. He had absolutely no right to take it.

As he got in his car, and this was just by chance that I ran into him, I walked up to his window and knocked on the glass signaling him to roll it down. I was kind of hoping he would be glad to see me but he wasn't, he was angry.

"What do you want?" he said with a look of disgust on his face as if he didn't even know me.

"I want my money that you stole from me," I said in a firm but gentle tone.

"GET," he snarled at me with a forward thrust, the way a dog would as if trying to bite you but being restrained causing an inability to reach, forcing me to take a step back and flinch. He then finished his sentence with "GET TAE ----!"

The last word my father would ever say to me was the most profane cuss word he knew.

Later in life, I reflected on that day as if to think what if things were different? What if we never moved here? What if? What if? What if? Was he just a product of his environment? Knowing his father and brother, I would say not. Was it something I did or said?

I would see him a couple times after that in passing when I would accompany my Mum to court while she was fighting for child support from him. He would never look at me. He would also never pay any type of support for his children and somehow the court let him get away with this. It was as if we never even existed in his eyes and he felt no remorse for leaving a wife and five children to fend for themselves.

## TOUGH TIMES GET TOUGHER

I spent that summer trying to do odd jobs to get some money. Covering other kid's paper routes, pumping gas or whatever I could find for a couple of dollars. My Mum started working two jobs. My older sister Lauren went to live with a friend of hers and dropped out of high school to work full time to support herself. I would visit her as much as I could.

We never had money. My Mum got on food stamps and my younger sister Catherine was in charge of getting the food with them once a month. Joanne would go to help carry them home most times or I would if needed. The electric bill and gas bill were always late. Catherine and I would walk to Newark, which was a full day roundtrip, to pay at the very last day before services were cut to save the few cents it would cost for the stamp.

We didn't have a washer and dryer in the apartment so we could only do laundry every other week when Mum got paid. Meanwhile, we would have to hand wash our clothes, the few that we had, in the sink and hang dry them on a clothes line in the summer or by the heater and oven in the winter.

Mum kept the food pantry cabinet locked with a padlock to ensure the food was rationed and nobody ate out of turn. We had no luxuries, like snacks or soda. We would make Kool-Aid in two gallon drink dispensers and we all thought it tasted terrible. That was because none of us knew we were supposed to add sugar to the mixture and none of us ever read the directions. I laugh about it now but it was horrible to live through.

We kids did everything around the house. Cook, clean, you name it. I missed reading as I had left behind all my books at my Dad's place. All my Mum had were Harlequin romance novels. She was an avid reader of these books. I tried reading one but could not get past the first couple chapters.

I played around in the kitchen, mostly trying to make foods that were cheap and filling. I would sometimes make pancakes for dinner or something that went well with rice. Rice was good because it was cheap and filling. Rice and beans, rice and chicken or just plain rice were staples. Pastas were also very common with generic brand canned sauce because that was cheaper than the jar sauces like Prego or Ragu.

Because I was in the kitchen so much it became my duty to do the dishes each day. I didn't mind that much, especially since all my sisters hated doing the dishes. I would have Catherine pick me up dry mixes to help bulk foods up by adding my own water. I would then start making casseroles with one of my favorite Goya Spanish seasoning packets. I would brown ground beef and cook off whatever macaroni noodles we had, mix them together, season and then bake in the oven for a few minutes to get the flavors incorporated.

By this time, I was starting high school and was working on choosing which classes I wanted to take. After selecting my mandatory math, English and science classes, I had to pick two electives to complete my schedule. I chose typing and introduction to cooking for the sole purpose that I assumed both these classes would be filled with girls and this would be a great chance for me to meet some girls.

The typing class was a great success. I was one of three boys in the class of thirty students. Cooking on the other hand was a bust. Not one girl in the whole class. I guess every other guy had the same idea.

But it was in the cooking class that I discovered how much I enjoyed cooking. I never really realized it at home, out of the sheer necessity of eating. To me it was either learn to cook or starve. But in this class, my eyes began to open, and I started to see cooking as more than just surviving.

I would still spend a lot of time in the library and started to enjoy the peace and quiet that I couldn't get anywhere else. Especially at home.

In an effort to make money, I asked my Uncle Tommy's partner Willie for a job doing whatever he needed done around the garage. My Uncle Tommy had left the business and went to work in a factory repairing production lines.

Right off the bat, Willie gave me a hard time for my long hair. I was just hoping he wasn't going to drag me to the barbers, as he did when we first met, and shave my head. He kindly gave me some grunt work to earn some money.

Willie wanted me to start right away and to be there immediately after school. I would walk the thirty minute walk to his garage from school at 2:30 in the afternoon, ready to clock in at 3:00 PM. I would work until 11 at night on weekdays, with most weekends off.

I was really grateful for the chance to work and extremely happy I was going to be making enough to start saving some money again. I was paid $103 after taxes each Friday and Willie was kind

67

enough to pay me the first week I started so I didn't have to wait until the following week to get paid. This was incredibly kind of him and I could see he felt sorry for me and my situation.

Willie's shop specialized in rebuilding car engines. The shop was littered with old junkers in the front, but inside the shop he had rooms full of parts, lifts and equipment to pull, clean and rebuild engines. My duty was to keep the shop clean and dip the engine parts into a caustic acid tank that would clean off all the dirt and grime accumulated on the outside and inside of the motors.

I didn't mind the work at all and was just happy to make the money. I enjoyed the walk from school each day. It helped me keep my sanity I think and allowed me the time to think since there was never peace and quiet at home to do so.

Each Saturday morning, I would go to the local diner with my Mum and buy her breakfast. Then I would give her $40 to help with the rent or however else she could use it. Our rent was $240 a month for a two bedroom dump that had no real privacy. Loud creaky stairs went up three flights with two apartments on each floor. You could hear televisions, chatter, arguing and even smell what everybody was cooking each day and there was only about two feet on each side separating the other buildings full of more people in the same crappy situation we were in.

What I liked most about working was I only had to go home to sleep. I was up each day at 6:30am to get ready, walk to school and get as much homework done as possible for the first four periods of class. The rest I did during lunch, which I never ate in school, or in easier classes I had later in the day.

I didn't have a social life to worry about since I felt that I never really fit into any social circles, and being a skinny ginger kid didn't help. I was picked on constantly and by now my hair was pretty long and not helping the situation. I had to give up all the activities and clubs that got me out of the house before working which didn't bother me since I was now enjoying the job I was doing and the interactions with Willie, his wife Catherine and the other employees at the shop.

Work ethic was one of the most valuable lessons I learned from Willie. He was tireless and had worked hard his whole life. This I knew by the way his hand would feel when shaking it. He had a hard tough skin and a grip like a vice with strong forearms and an insatiable appetite for an excuse to use them. The calluses on his hands were like nail heads sticking out of a piece of wood. They were hard to the touch and well aged, protruding into your hand as if to leave indentations from his firm grip. He was always dressed in the standard blue work shirt and trousers with the sleeves rolled up ready to take on the world. Willie was loud and boisterous with a quick wit and a banter that could go on forever. He loved what he did and it showed in the care he took of the customer's vehicles he worked on. The results of a job can always be reflected by the care that goes into it.

I would still laugh at the "In God We Trust, All Others Cash" sign in the office just as I did when I first arrived in America.

Willie was tremendous in helping me shed the boy and become the man. He was like a drill sergeant in a lot of ways, not just to me but to everybody in the shop.

"David," he would say in a loud authoritative voice, "go get me the heads for this engine."

I would do my best to get done whatever he would ask for as quickly as possible, because as soon as you turned from him he would snap into "C'mon man move your ----. Quicker, quicker, c'mon you're too slow." I would be running my tail off and still he would push for more. The pressure was hard to bear some days but it would be funny to listen to the American guys working there saying things like, "Who's this guy think he is? He can't talk to me like that."

It was incredibly funny. There were a few guys that wouldn't last a week. When Willie would yell, everybody would jump. Nobody would say anything to his face for fear of getting torn into by him in a way that would make you cry and I was scared to death of him. That fear kept me sharp and on my toes every night.

Nobody knew if he was ever in the Army, but I would bet he had to have been, given how hard he could push you to your limits.

I started to save my money for clothes each week and also bought my own tools to work with in the shop instead of borrowing the other mechanics' tools and listening to them complain that if you want to be a mechanic you need to buy your own tools. My answer was always the same, that I didn't want to be a mechanic so can I borrow your mechanic tools please?

I eventually cut my hair and kept it short so Willie would stop giving me a hard time about it. My grades started slipping in school due to the long work weeks and I eventually ended up leaving the garage to focus on what I would do as a career. I had decided to pursue a career in cooking at the age of fifteen. I figured I enjoyed that more than being anything else and started looking for opportunities to cook.

I already had some good experience from high school and went around to local restaurants to fill out applications.

Nobody took me serious until I met Shep.

Prior to meeting Shep, I started to cut some classes at school, take the PATH train to New York City's World Trade Center station and walk around reading the menus that restaurants would post near their doors in an effort to entice prospective diners to patronize the establishment.

I loved the smells from restaurant to restaurant as I would bounce around from one to the other. I didn't have a lot of money so I couldn't eat in any of the fancier restaurants. But I would go to whichever one I thought was reasonable, nurse a cup of coffee and watch the plates as they came out.

My favorite places to go though were the restaurants in Chinatown. I could stand there for hours watching the cooks perform their ballet of sorts over the endless row of woks without missing a beat. Those guys, in my opinion, were the masters. They would effortlessly push and pull the water valves on and off above their woks with the bamboo handled mesh stirrers that they would use to sauté the most aromatic foods I had ever smelled. The sesame scent was irresistible and the way they would listen to the orders being what seemed like screamed at them from the ladies working the front impressed me the most, especially as hot as the place would be. It was so hot that they could grow banana trees in there, especially since it was a moist heat with billows of steam reaching for the stained drop ceiling squares that had seen much better days. But these guys were cool under pressure and had a swagger all of their own. The ladies up

71

front would work the phones, the register and the fryers, while each cook had a cart of 'mise en place' next to them with what seemed like endless ingredients.

I never noticed any mistakes or burns happening. It was as if every move was rehearsed over and over again and only the top flight cooks could be seen by the impatient punters standing in queue acting as if these guys were working too slowly. Could you imagine if Willie was there? And the slower guys were the ones sitting around the back table cleaning the stems off of the green beans.

There were also Italian places. I would watch the Italian pizza makers, hand tossing their dough in the showcase window. As if watching some guy roll his dough around his hairy arms would entice you to eat there but what did I know? I would have loved to have the talent these guys had.

All I could think of while walking around was how lucky I was to be so close to all this action. I would walk down to Battery Park on occasion and feel like Holden Caulfield sitting on a park bench watching the cast of characters parade by on their way to whatever they decided to do with their lives.

I loved the bustle of the city and there always seemed to be a lot going on with everybody in such a hurry to wherever they had to be ten minutes ago. The people, for the most part, were rude and I wondered why a lot of the guys would talk so tough and forceful in even the simplest of conversations but I didn't let that stop me from interacting. I knew I was the one who was different and as much a foreigner as the other immigrants around town trying to make their way in the world for a better life. The only difference was I felt the better life was back home in Scotland.

As impressed as I was with all the different styles of restaurants there were in the city, I never had the courage to try to get a job cooking there for fear of being way out of my league. I stuck to my side of the river, in the minor leagues, in hopes of learning how to master the culinary arts before moving up to compete in this market. I kept applying to the local restaurants in hopes somebody would take a chance on me but nobody ever called back. I even applied to the very small Chinese restaurant two blocks from our apartment only to be laughed at by the counter help. They probably thought I was joking but I was dead serious. I wanted to learn how to cook like these guys.

I met Shep through a friend of mine who had scored a job at a bakery through a vocational work study program. They were looking for one other kid to help, so my friend called me knowing that I would be interested since it meant working with food. I excitedly went to the bakery the next morning and met with the guy running things. Shep.

Shep was a tough guy on the exterior with arms as big as my legs and the form of an old school boxer. He stood about 6' 2" even hunched over, with long curly brown hair and pork chop sideburns. He kind of reminded me of Tom Jones. He was Jewish and wore a gold pendant of a Hebrew symbol around his thick neck. Shep openly said he was in no mood to deal with crap, although his word choice was more colorful, so if I wanted to work here I would need to show up every day on time and come prepared to work.

"Strong backs and weak minds is what I need," he said while flicking his ashes into the trash can next to the coffee maker as we stood in an office reception area that was outdated by about twenty years. He went on to tell me he wasn't looking for any part-time kids that were going to complain all day and be a pain in his rear end, as he puffed away on a cigarette with one hand and stirred a cup of coffee with the other hand.

I was unprepared for this because by now I was sixteen years old and heading into my senior year of high school from a stellar academic junior year where, even though I cut a lot of classes, I made honor roll. He made me feel that if I had said no thanks that I would have been found guilty of committing high treason and shot at dawn. But, I really needed the money.

My Mum had spent part of the summer in the hospital with an irregular heart beat from stress and working two jobs full time and managing the household on her own. I needed to bring some money in to keep her from going back to two jobs and I feared the worst would happen if she did. All these thoughts were going through my head at once. Without thinking I said, "I'm your man, I won't let you down."

I didn't know what I was in for. I hardly knew anything about baking and wanted to be a chef not a baker. I wanted to wear a fancy white jacket, a fancy white hat and flame thirty things in sauté pans at once while yelling at the waiters to get the food out while it was hot and stop complaining about the plates being too hot to touch. All I knew about baking was one time I made an apple pie in school and almost cut my finger off. I hadn't a clue what to expect.

Now by telling Shep I was his man meant I gave my word that I would not let him down. Afterwards, I had this overwhelming feeling of guilt and was trying to figure out what I was going to do next month when school started back up.

Even though I was excited about getting a job, I was still trying to justify in my head that I did the right thing and I shouldn't worry about next month yet. Maybe Shep would think I'm a worthless immigrant with no business in his bakery should I screw up within the first couple of days of my pathetic excuse for baking and all this worry will be for naught.

The very next morning I got a ride to the bakery from another guy who lived near by and who had also just started at the bakery. When I arrived I didn't know what to expect. I walked in through the loading dock door and saw piles and piles of one hundred pound bags of flour and sugar. Pails of jelly and fruit fillings and racks upon racks of every type of baked good you could imagine. My first order of business was to seek out Shep and find out what he wanted me to do. I wasn't nervous, just overwhelmed by all the equipment and hustle and bustle of the cadence on the floor. Hot racks out while cold racks get loaded up to go into the biggest oven I had ever seen in my life. I was completely lost.

Shep was standing hunched over an old wooden work bench hand depositing what looked like a batter onto sheet trays piled about twenty high and to my amazement every deposit was exactly uniform by him pushing the batter up through the cup of his left hand and sweeping it off with the paddle he called his right hand. Now I knew why he was always hunched over. Probably spending more than forty years in the same position. All I could think was, "I hope I don't end up like this."

He had a cigarette burning on the edge of the work bench which looked to be in its place by the sight of all the cigarette burns standing like little soldiers along three quarters the length of the table. It's funny because the first thought I had was each of these burns probably represented a smart mouth high schooler getting his rear end kicked every day until he quit for a softer job that didn't require muscles.

"I'll show you where the aprons are and then I need you to work in the packing room until they get caught up and then you get in the kitchen and wash all the dirty pans in the sink area. Sound good?" he said while finishing what batter he had in hand then headed to the sink.

The work wasn't bad and the time seemed to fly by that first day. I kept my mouth shut and tried very hard to impress Shep.

The smell of the bakery wowed me. There was this sweet melody of smells that permeated through the air almost hypnotizing my subconscious into a submissive state of joy that reminded me immediately of a story I read a few years back. The book of Exodus, the second book of Moses, chapter twenty nine, verse forty. God was instructing Moses on the ordination of Aaron and one of the daily offerings was flour mixed with oil because the odor pleases God. "Fascinating," I thought, because I could now relate to why this would be pleasing to God and found the first connection I would have with food. Its sense of pleasing.

Before I only looked at food in the sense of sustainability. There were foods I liked, fish and chips, meat pies and beans, sliced sausage and rasher bacon, Mars bars, salt and vinegar crisps, toast and tea, jam sandwiches and fruit yogurt. There were far more foods I hated, like, for example, my Mums cooking. She's a terrible cook but an outstanding baker. Her clootie dumpling (a traditional Scottish pudding) is the best I have ever had and her tablet was divine. Tablet is basically a hardened sugar caramel and dumpling is a boiled sweet cake with currents and suet boiled to perfection and absolutely the best dessert pudding in the world.

Mum's Sunday roasts on the other hand were dreaded by me every week and probably the reason I didn't eat steak for years to come because I thought it was all that bad. Mum's was so dry the proteins would shred when you cut it and there was never a gravy to help it down. The salt would bounce off of the meat as if trying to escape. There were no juices to absorb the salt. It was so well done that it was grey and she would always make mashed potatoes with it. Her mashed potatoes were so dry and lumpy that I used to put them in my trouser pockets with ease in order to evade eating them. After I would leave the table I would pitch them outside the way the prisoners in the great escape did while carrying out the dirt from the tunnel they were building to escape the German POW camp. Mum's potatoes were awful. To this day, I cannot eat mashed potatoes because it gives me a gag complex that is uncontrollable. I can eat potatoes every way but mashed.

One day, before my Dad had left us, I was in such a hurry to get back outside to play football that when I ran out the door after dinner I forgot to dump the potatoes out of my pocket. Mum found them while doing laundry and Dad was more than happy to teach me a lesson and encourage me to never do that again.

Working in the packing room allowed me the opportunity to learn all the different baked goods we produced and how best to handle them when done. The bakery specialized in supplying a lot of restaurants and entertainment venues in New York with a wide variety of specialty baked goods. We made layer cakes of all varieties, cookies, pies, strudels, hamentashen, almond horns, babka and snack cakes.

Every day I was learning something new. After about three weeks, Shep pulled me aside while I was on my way to the pot sink to wash up the pans and bowls.

"Hey Dave," he said

"Oh great," I thought, "Here it comes. I am working too slow and he's about to kick me out of here on my rear end. I will probably end up going back to Willie's boot camp with my tail between my legs having not being able to handle the food business." I thought for sure I was doomed.

"Don't worry about the pots today," he said as he was lighting a fresh cigarette with another one that was about to burn out. "Stay in packing. The guys said you're doing a great job back there and I got a new guy coming in to take over the porter duties so consider this your first promotion."

I was ecstatic. My first promotion! Wow, what a feeling! I went from making $3.25 an hour to $3.50. You would have thought he handed me the keys to a new car. I couldn't believe it.

After thanking Shep, I headed back to the packing room and smiled the whole rest of the day. I had thought for sure I was toast. In a way, I was kind of hoping I was because it was time to head to school next week and I was too scared to give in my notice. I procrastinated over doing so, not just out of fear of getting yelled at or anything like that but I didn't want to let anybody down. Everybody that started work around the time I did had already quit and I didn't think I would make it this far. I was enjoying what I was doing and, with them leaving, I was getting a lot of overtime. This was all going into my savings, since Shep paid me cash for any hours over forty.

I still took my Mum to breakfast each Saturday morning and she was glad to see me happy at what I was doing and encouraged me to stick with it.

"Chefs make good money you know," she would say. Our Saturday morning breakfast was the only quiet time we could spend together and was a way that I could thank her for getting us this far. It wasn't easy taking care of all of us kids, especially in a foreign country with no help from our Dad. She encouraged me to do good in life and not to let the circumstances we were living in drive me to choose a life of crime, which could have been easy to do, in order to be successful but rather work hard for everything I wasn't given. My Mum was very supportive of me for choosing a career. The only thing we disagreed on was that I needed to be happy doing what I chose to do to make money. Her outlook was that nobody was ever happy working. They are only happy for the money so try to make as much money as you can.

It was time for me to make a decision on whether to stay at the bakery or go back to school and get my diploma. Although I didn't want to let Shep down, first and foremost I didn't want to let my Mum down either. She couldn't afford for me to stop working and do

79

without forty percent of my pay. I didn't want her to have to work two jobs again just to end up in the hospital. My deadbeat Dad wasn't going to subsidize any of our expenses, he was too caught up in his own life and had married the woman he was dating after the divorce was final.

I decided to stay on working and figure out how to get my diploma later. The money right then meant more to us as a family than a stupid piece of paper that could only help me get into another school, that I couldn't afford anyway, just to get another piece of paper. I was well educated, mostly due to my own determination, so I didn't think risking giving up my job would do any of us any good at all.

A month into my senior year of high school and two months before my seventeenth birthday, I received a letter from the high school basically asking me what my intentions were. If I did not reply or show up for class they would consider that as a drop out and close my school record.

"Well, close it," I thought. It wasn't like they were sending a letter because they missed me.

Overall, I think I made the right decision. It wasn't long before Shep moved me out of packaging and into baking. He took me under his wing and taught me everything I know about the science of baking and this proved to be invaluable since most chefs have no idea how to bake, making me more valuable. I owe all of that to him and think of him every time I have baked products from that day of my career to this day.

I was his apprentice and he was a great teacher. Even though I could only carry one bag of flour or sugar to his two, he never complained or told me I wasn't doing well. He always encouraged me and shared a lot of his time for me to learn the trade.

He taught me how to mix doughs, sheet doughs, understand how to work with yeast, deposit, bake and decorate cakes. He made me roll out puff pastry by hand instead of using the machine to incorporate the fat into the dough. He taught me how to roll and proof danish, how to incorporate flavor into a glaze and most of all how to be a professional. He taught me how to use my hands, "The best tools God gave you," he would say.

Shep turned out to be sort of a father figure to me in passing down a tradition. He had swagger, class and a ton of knowledge that I worked tirelessly to extract from his brain. He walked like all the other old timers in the bakery, hunched over with thick swinging arms like a bear, that would take your head off should the need arise. His hands were as thick as the oven mitts I used to handle the hot pans with and seemed to be heat resistant. Pulling hot trays out of the rack and checking the bounce on the layer cakes to ensure they were done properly looked easy and effortless for him to do bare handed.

The rumor in the bakery was that Shep had spent quite a few years in prison for murder. I couldn't say whether this was true or not and I never dared to ask him. He turned out to be pretty cool toward me so I didn't care if he did or not. It was none of my business.

Funny thing was that one of Shep's daughters, from one of his many marriages, was going to visit him down here from Albany and she was third runner up for Miss New York the year prior. We were all very excited to have a beauty queen visit our rag tag bunch of social misfits.

Shep rounded us all up in the kitchen and said, "My daughter is going to be here with me tomorrow night for a couple hours before we drive out to Long Island for the weekend. Any of you ------- get any smart ideas and try anything stupid with my daughter, I will kill you. Got it?"

We were shaking in our boots. Everybody nodded yes and didn't say a word until he walked away. We were left standing there knowing for sure this guy would kill us. Heck, he was already a convicted killer, supposedly, and none of us wanted to test the waters and see if it was true.

This guy would pick up eighty quart mixing bowls with one hand without even the ash from the cigarette hanging in his mouth dropping to the ground. There was no way I was even going to think about crossing him.

When Shep's daughter arrived we were afraid to look at her. We made sure the kitchen was clean and we actually put some effort, for once, in making sure we looked good in our bakery whites. She was every bit as beautiful as we could imagine a beauty queen to look like but it was like meeting The Queen. Nobody looked her in the eye.

We didn't want Shep to take a detour off the drive to Long Island to unload one of our stiff carcasses in his trunk in the Meadowlands now did we?

She must have thought we were a bunch of rude dummies with some kind of anti-social disorder acting as if she wasn't even in the building or speaking a foreign language.

After about two hours, of what seemed like an eternity for everybody being on such good behavior, I think even Shep couldn't handle it anymore. Shep had had enough and packed it in for the weekend. He rolled up his apron, picked up the four packs of cigarettes that seemed to always be on his bench and headed out without any of us stuffed in the trunk of his Cadillac. Thank goodness.

Everybody was going nuts waiting for him to leave and checking the coast was clear before saying a word.

For the rest of the night all we could talk about was Shep's daughter and how beautiful she looked even from our peripheral vision and ways in which Shep would kill us. We laughed for hours.

I decided after that night, and since I had enough money, to ask my Mum if I could buy a plane ticket to fly home for the first time since landing in America. She didn't have a problem with it and neither did Shep so I decided to go home for my seventeenth birthday for a couple of days. It was the best decision I had ever made up to that time and was long overdue in my opinion.

## HEADED HOME

I left for Scotland in the early part of November 1984, from JFK airport in New York. I was excited to venture out on my own and very much looking forward to the trip. It was an evening departure flight that was due to land in Ireland around six in the morning and then off to Prestwick airport in Ayrshire, Scotland, arriving four hours later at around ten.

My Uncle Vinny and his wife Pat picked me up at the airport and I was so excited to see them for the simple reason that it verified that I was home. It was a beautiful morning with the sun shining and it felt absolutely great to see the countryside scenery on the way to Port Glasgow, where they are from.

My Mum's family is from Port Glasgow, which sits on the banks of the River Clyde facing to the north. The town wasn't famous for much except its hard-working, working-class people who worked the shipyards on the docks and the factories in the Devol area.

The heyday of the shipyards was from the 1800s to World War II. All the males in my Mum's family worked at either the shipyards or the ammunition factory in the late 1930s and early 1940s, unless of course they were serving in the Army. By 1984, most of the shipyards were closed and the town had an extremely high unemployment rate, especially among the men both old and young.

Port Glasgow is a very picturesque town because of its location. When you look out over the Clyde you can see the foothills of the Grampian Mountains and the head and shoulders of Ben Lomond. In November, the mountains are frosted with snow and blend beautifully with the dark base, contrasting grey sides and frosted tops reaching into an endless fluff of clouds which never seem to disappear.

The Port sits about ten miles west of Glasgow with a replica of the PS Comet (the first steam ship in Europe built by Henry Bell) sitting proudly in the center of town, next to the River Clyde. The Clyde was the main artery connecting Glasgow with every other corner of the earth that has been touched by the great people of Scotland.

We had stopped for some tea at a cafe along the way to catch up on the past six years I had been in America. My Uncle Vinny wasn't at all surprised to hear what my Dad had done to us. He asked me if I wanted to go to the pub that night if I was up to it and I said absolutely.

After reaching their house and getting reacquainted with their five children, we had some dinner and then headed off to the pub. It was great. My Uncle John met us there and he looked exactly the same way he did when he saw us off to America six years before.

The pub was called The Wallace. It sat right on Parkhill Avenue facing the apartment tenements where my Mum was born. It was named The Wallace after William Wallace. There was a tree not far down the road that had supposedly been where William Wallace was chained after he was captured, before being sent to England to face execution.

Most of the tree had concrete around the base in what looked like an effort to maintain its integrity. Chains had been imbedded in part of the concrete and made to look as if they were the original chains that bound a hero in Scottish history.

It was great to be back in Scotland. I was so happy and it felt like the first time I had been happy in my whole life.

Uncle Vinny is an avid Celtic fan so my Uncle John, Uncle Vinny and I went to a game at Celtic Park in the Parkhead area of Glasgow.

There are two premier football teams in Glasgow. Celtic is the team of the Irish Catholic immigrants that settled in Scotland to work during the famine of Ireland. Rangers is the protestant team of native Glaswegians that were loyal to King William of Orange and opposed the Catholic doctrine.

Personally, I think both teams are great teams. I never cared for the sectarian violence that has taken place between opposing fans, and that has caused a huge riff between the people of Glasgow.

IT'S A GAME!

My Granddad, from my Dad's side of the family, was a Rangers fan. My Mum's family are Celtic fans. This means, in Glasgow, I am the product of a mixed marriage.

Fights break out continuously and there are even deaths associated with "wearing the wrong color." It is all such unnecessary nonsense, in my honest opinion. This is the ugly side of football that I dislike most. We should share in the success of both teams and forget about the stupidity of hating people because they don't see the world the same way we do!

After the game, we headed to the pub to watch the highlights of the game we just saw live. We had a few pints of some of the most delicious beer in the world and talked until around eleven at night.

I enjoyed a week of all my favorite foods, being around my favorite people and started to feel whole again. I was dreading going back to America, and inside I was wishing there was a way I could stay.

My cousin, Vivian, accompanied me to Glasgow to spend a day in the city. We had a great time together. She is Uncle Vinny's oldest daughter. I ate two fish suppers that day and we must have gone into every shop along Buchanan Street. We didn't make it back until late that evening. We ended up at my cousin Catherine and her husband Robert's house. Catherine and I became great friends through the years and I visited her every chance I got. Catherine and her husband Robert died tragically in a house fire several years later on the same day I married my wife Christina. I miss them both very much to this day.

My Mum had given me a shopping list of items I had to take back with me and I spent a whole day going from shop to shop to fill the list. Before I knew it, it was time to fly back to America and get back to work in order to save enough money to return by Spring. An achievement that I was determined to accomplish, and an achievement I did.

Upon my return to Kearny, I got a phone call that the bakery I worked in had burned down. I couldn't believe my luck. I knew I should have stayed in Scotland.

So I didn't need to go into work the next day after I got back and tried to put a strategy together for what I was going to do next. I wasn't in the mood to go job hunting right away but it had to be done. I headed down to the corner store to get the paper and start thumbing through the classifieds for whatever job would take a chance on me again.

The next day I got a call from Terri who was the front office manager for the bakery I worked at.

"Macfarlane," she said in that strong authoritative tone she had as if calling one of her children to the carpet for acting up in school, "Are you back from your vacation?"

I couldn't help but laugh, "Of course I am, you called me at my house in Kearny."

"Well you need to get down here to the bakery 'cause you're supposed to work, remember?" Terri said back.

"I thought it burned down?" I said puzzled. "I was told it burned down."

"Just get here as quick as possible all right dumb ---." She loved the use of affectionate profanity.

After a quick bus ride to Lyndhurst, I arrived at the bakery to find out what was going on. It was owned by Ron and Joe Aihini, a father and son from Long Island City, New York. They couldn't help but laugh when I showed up and I thought there was a joke being played on me. After we all had a good laugh and they said they were happy to see me they filled me in on what was going on.

While I was in Scotland, the bakery had their annual inspection from the rabbi who would certify them Kosher. During this certification, the rabbi also blesses the bakery and all the equipment. While blessing the oven he put some unleavened bread in at the highest temperature the oven would go to and, as a result, the floorboards underneath the oven caught fire.

The rest of the bakery was fine. Just the production area where the ovens were had to be totally redone but we were continuing on by using another bakery's kitchen during the rebuild process.

The other bakery was in Newark and closer to our apartment so I was happy about that. The only thing that would be difficult was that after baking everything we would then have to pack it and truck it back to Lyndhurst, since that was the distribution center as well as where the route drivers would pick up their orders before heading into New York City.

To me, this was pretty good news all around since I needed the job and, with the change in the production schedule, it meant I would get a ton of overtime. Which I needed, after spending so much money at home.

I worked so hard over the next few months that I didn't even have time to miss Scotland nor have time to go to night school to get my diploma. I was now seventeen and I had to start thinking about going to culinary school to fulfill my dream of being a chef.

When things got back to normal, and our bakery kitchen was rebuilt, I was back to working my normal hours. I went from 74 hours a week back down to 60. This hurt financially a little bit but it was nice to have a life again. I went back to my old habits of visiting New York, growing my hair out and playing around in the kitchen at home. Something I hadn't done in a long time.

When I was in cooking class in high school, we had a chef visit from the Culinary Institute of America in Hyde Park, NY. It was regarded as the premier culinary school in the world and what impressed me most was that they didn't accept any new students that had less than two years experience in the food industry. It would take me two more years to finish my apprenticeship in the bakery so the plan was to visit the school, find out how much it was and prepare to enroll after I had completed my work at the bakery.

Time was on my side. If I saved my money for school, I thought, I should be ready in two years time.

After a visit to the campus, and being wowed by the sheer size of the school, I was ready to sign up that day. Trouble was, I had to wait until I was a baker. Once the tour was complete, I got all the information I needed and then the incredibly sad news that this school was way out of my price range. I could never afford to go there.

A student loan was an option but I remembered what Willie had taught me about credit.

"If you canny afford it, then you're not meant to have it." Basically, don't go into debt.

At first I was trying to justify to myself that I deserved to go there and that it was normal to take out a student loan for a world class education. "I should be making enough when I graduate to pay back the loan in record time and still live comfortably right?"

Who was I kidding? I couldn't afford it and when I really thought about it, it didn't make any sense to go into debt in order to get a job to pay the debt. I already had a job. What would I do that for?

I was confused. So I turned my attention to the bakery and figured I would figure things out later.

Before I knew it, I was on a plane back to Scotland for another holiday. I waited until the summer, since I found a better deal to fly into London and take the train up to Glasgow, rather than fly direct.

It was a great summer.

Ron, the owner of the bakery, was in Scotland for a couple days as part of a tour he was on with his wife and another couple. We spent the day together, sailing on Loch Lomond, touring Edinburgh Castle, touring Rabbie Burns' Cottage and shopping on High Street. It was a great time and I loved being around Ron. He was old school. A hard working businessman that came up through the ranks with nothing. Everything he had, he earned. And that impressed me.

Ron would listen to self help and motivational cassette tapes wherever he would go. He would call himself "The Great One." Ron drove a new Cadillac every year and always dressed like he was about to get inaugurated as the President of the United States. Ron was a classy guy and it showed.

It was great to spend some time with Ron outside of work. He was a hard guy to work for but he was always fair and he expected the very best out of his underlings. What boss doesn't? Ron always wanted me to start reading business books, which was something I never cared for that much. I wasn't into the Wall Street type of life and thought most of those guys were corrupt and straight up thieves who took pleasure in getting over on somebody in order to make themselves wealthy. Money never meant that much to me.

I took his advice and read Donald Trump's "The Art of the Deal" after I left the bakery. Overall, it was a decent story but still not my cup of tea. I was into reading cookbooks and only cookbooks by now.

With the ability to work and travel back home on occasion, I started to feel a little better about myself. Home life was getting better but was still hard. Mum got a new job that paid more but it was still factory work. Dad was a distant, bad memory and I never wondered how he was doing. I sincerely gave up caring about him, finally.

Time seemed to be flying by and before long I was eighteen. I had finally got my driver's license although I'd been driving for a year. I used to help out with deliveries in the city for anybody that needed help for extra money. One of the bakeries in Long Island City would let me drive deliveries in the city on my days off for some extra side money.

I still needed to figure out culinary school. I didn't have the means to support myself and I was still against taking out a loan. So, I decided to look into what the US Navy had available, since they had a reputation for putting out some really good cooks.

There was a recruiting office in Kearny and it seemed to be a pretty busy little place. Why not, there were plenty of kids looking to get out of that town.

Petty Officer Chris Shrubsall was the recruiter and he was more than happy to share with me what to expect if I decided to join up as a Navy cook. After sifting through the first hour of how great Navy life was and how I would be doing a great service by joining, I put the breaks on his sales pitch. I told him what I was really there for. I just wanted to go to culinary school, so what was available?

Chris went on to tell me the procedure for taking my ASVAB test, getting a physical and, based on the results of my test, to see if I qualify for Mess Management Specialist School in San Diego. The catch was that I had to score over fifty on my exam in order to qualify without a high school diploma.

That weekend I went to the book store and picked up a book to help me study for my exam. Within a couple weeks I was ready for my test.

Chris turned out to be a pretty cool guy. He was a career sailor and had been around the world more times than he cared to count. He even did a tour aboard ship stationed in Scotland. He opened up to me about a lot of the crap you have to put up with in the service and was proud of his accomplishments in the Navy. This was his first shore duty and he was on his last tour before retiring. Chris wasn't going to get promoted to Chief, so he was getting out at his 20 year mark.

When he drove me for my testing in Newark he wished me luck and said he'd pick me up after my physical and interview tomorrow. If all went well then I was to swear in on that next day and await orders to leave for boot camp.

I ended up scoring an 82 on my exam and had no problem going in as a cook after the interviewer decided I was a lost cause to try to convince to join under a more technical job that matched my test results. I was only set on going to cooking school so I stuck to my guns.

The hardest part of the physical was that I was one pound under weight. I was a little, skinny guy and even though I was lifting hundred pound sacks of flour every day you would never tell by looking at me. The guy checking my weight just looked at me and said I was under weight and should try gaining some weight then come back. I was disappointed and just looked to the floor. No matter how much I ate I could never gain weight. He must have felt sorry for me then he marked his sheet with an added pound and said good luck. I was smiling from ear to ear.

I swore in that day and patiently waited for Chris outside the MEPS building. After he decided to show up and I got in the car, I tried to look disappointed and told him they wouldn't take me. He couldn't believe me and thought it was because of my test score. After he was racking his brain for a way to remedy the problem I caved in and pulled my packet out from behind my jacket. He was back to his normal self and then dropped me off at home. I had six months to wait to leave for boot camp, so had plenty of time to go home to Scotland for a quick trip and finish at the bakery.

## ANCHORS AWEIGH

On an especially chilly morning on November 10, 1986, I left New Jersey for sunny San Diego, California, to attend Recruit Training. Then, upon completion, I was to go to Mess Management A School, San Diego.

I was especially excited to see the West Coast for the first time and was looking forward to whatever fate awaited me. When I arrived at the Military Entrance Processing Station in Newark it was around 6:30 in the morning. I was there until four in the afternoon doing absolutely nothing. Just sitting in a room, with about 20 other guys, and none of us had a clue what to expect. Finally, I was handed my orders for San Diego and two plane tickets. One to Denver and the other from Denver to San Diego. I was due to arrive there at midnight.

I was given taxi fare and told to head to the airport. If I didn't report to San Diego at the specified arrival time and place then I would be in violation of some uniform code of some kind and hunted down to face prison. I thought it was funny how all of a sudden I could commit a criminal offense when I was the one who volunteered to do this. I am sure some people get second thoughts but I thought the way I was talked to was completely unnecessary.

When I eventually arrived in San Diego I was tired. I slept a little on the flight in from Denver but it was so turbulent that it was hard to sleep as much as I wanted to.

After walking through the airport and going outside, I couldn't believe how warm it was considering how bitter cold it was in Jersey when I left. It was the first time I had ever seen palm trees. So far, I liked this. All I needed now was for the Wiki bus to come pick me up and take me to my resort on the beach.

Other guys started straggling down to the entrance of the airport with vanilla envelopes in hand just like mine and none of us had a clue if we were going to be picked up or if we were going to need a taxi or what to do.

Before long this guy in his Navy whites walked around the corner and almost directly into me as we almost collided. I asked him if he knew what I was supposed to do, as I was reporting into boot camp. He glanced up at me, he was really short, and gave me a look of disgust as if I just asked him where Olive Oil was.

"Get your --- out of my way and over to the bus stop you stupid blankety, blankety, blank," he screamed at me and pointed to the side of the building where there was a white school bus at the curb.

"Oh great, here we go," is what I thought to myself as I headed to the bus as quick as I could. The drive to the base seemed like it was only a block away. We could have walked there it was so short.

Now my first impression upon arriving at the training center and being told to sit on the blue square tile and only the blue square tile was, to be completely honest, that I thought there had been a mistake with what Navy I joined.

Every one of the drill instructors that were there were Filipino and extremely hard to understand. I didn't know what to make of this. It took every bone in my body to keep from raising my hand and asking what the heck is going on here? Did I join the wrong Navy? But, I was afraid of getting myself in trouble.

Turns out, the US had a relationship with the Philippines after World War II that allowed Filipinos to join the armed forces. Most of them joined the Navy because of the presence the Navy had in the Philippines, without having to immigrate to the US first.

Once this was explained to us by our company commander, Chief Petty Officer McIntyre and Petty Officer First Class Damasco, I thought that it was pretty cool that they were able to join the Navy. They were no different than me in the pursuit of bettering ourselves, so I accepted them as my comrades and appreciated getting to know a lot of them as true friends throughout my naval career and after.

Boot camp was a breeze. I never had to think. I was told how to do everything from folding my clothes to how to carry the old out-of-date M1 rifles we toted everywhere we went. Run, eat, sleep and swim was all we did it seemed like. The weather was the best weather I had ever witnessed and for the eight weeks I spent in boot camp you couldn't have asked for it to be more perfect.

The food, as you may remember I am a finicky eater, was completely foreign to me. Stuffed peppers with ground beef and rice, Creole chicken, chili macaroni and a lot of sides I had never seen before like collard greens, okra, and red beans and rice.

Being the cautious eater that I was, with a fear of getting sick especially when running, I stuck to a diet that was familiar, simple and filling.

For breakfast every morning, I would have four peanut butter sandwiches and black coffee. Lunch and dinner were just as simple, peanut butter and jelly sandwiches, how many depended on how hungry I was, black coffee and salad. I never deviated from this menu and besides, we only had about ten minutes to eat so I stuck with what was familiar. I did not want to waste food by loading up on food I had never tried before. I didn't want to wind up hating it and throwing it away.

After graduating boot camp and reporting to the training center for school, the first meal I ate was chicken parmesan. Heavenly, I thought.

I could hardly contain my excitement when starting cooking school. This was finally the moment I was waiting for and all I could focus on for two years. Most of the instructors were Filipino and by now I understood their accents easily which helped me from preventing mistakes in my work and lessons.

The first day was spent in a lab where each student was given a cutting board, chef's knife and some vegetables. After being shown how to handle the knife, we were instructed to copy the cuts of the vegetables that our teacher demonstrated and place our waste in an insert pan next to the cutting board so he could evaluate how much waste we were producing and whether or not we used the vegetables to the highest yield possible. For the first time I was demonstrating, in a professional kitchen, how I had been practicing vegetable cuts and I took great care not to waste the vegetables.

Working in the bakery had taught me a lot about waste. In any efficient food operation it can raise your production costs and deplete from your profits if it gets out of hand. Shep taught me how that sometimes mistakes can be made but you cannot let them overtake your productivity. He taught me how to make brownies and crumb (an essential part of constructing layer cakes) with pressing crumb around the walls of the cake for decoration, out of cakes that didn't turn out good enough to sell. He taught me how to manage my waste and if I make mistakes then I needed to correct what I did wrong and not to let it happen again.

School for a Mess Management Specialist was eight weeks long and very intense. I didn't just learn how to cook but learned how to cook on a ship. We used shipboard equipment and worked off of the AFRS (Armed Forces Recipe Service) which were step-by-step index cards of all the recipes used in the Navy for ship and shore feeding. We couldn't work with open flame on a ship so we focused on steam jacketed kettles, griddles, ovens, deep fat fryers and steamers. Soups, gravies, stews and any other wet foods were prepared in the kettles and an important part of shipboard feeding.

The hardest part that I had to learn was eggs to order on a hot griddle and cooking about seven to ten orders at a time. As people would go through the line you had to ask how they wanted their eggs and make them as fast as possible. On my first day doing this, I was completely nervous. It was incredibly important to have enough eggs on station and have all your ingredients like grated cheese, diced ham, diced onion, diced peppers and so on at close reach. It was also important to work fast and clean. Nobody liked to get a sloppy omelet or broken yolks if they ordered over-easy eggs. After a couple of times working the egg section, I became more and more confident and learned how to establish a system so I would work fast and not make any mistakes by giving the wrong order on the wrong tray as they passed by.

I always took great pride in my work and I wasn't going to let this beat me. So when we were going through our morning assignments, and if the Chief asked who wanted to work eggs, I was always the first to raise my hand. This took a lot of pressure off everybody else because nobody ever wanted to do it. It was the hardest job on the breakfast line and all eyes were on whoever was making the eggs.

A couple of weeks in, and it was time for baking class. I was not too eager for this class except for the fact that I would be making donuts for the first time. The bakery I worked in didn't have donuts nor a fryer so I was looking forward to cutting and frying some dough.

On the first night, I was assigned to make sheet cakes, icings, brownies, muffins and pies. All the things I had done a million times before. I was disappointed that I didn't get the donut job but figured I'd get it eventually. Unwittingly, I took charge of completing our list of baked goods with the three other students in my group. I showed them how to read the recipes, mix, deposit by hand the way Shep taught me, bake and check the doneness of each item.

By the end of the night and after cleaning up I proceeded to the storeroom to grab bags of flour to refill the white roller bins that were kept underneath each work bench. I never bothered to ask for help and I was doing exactly what I was trained to do in the bakery I just spent three years in.

Take the lids off the bins and pull the scoops out. Wash the scoops and set to dry. Put two bins side by side. Place the bag on top off both bins, cut open and dump materials in proper labeled bins. The reason you place two bins together is to support the bag while you cut it open then lift the bag into the empty bin.

Nobody had asked me to fill the bins, it is just something I did instinctively but proved to be an almost fatal mistake.

Who the ---- filled these bins?" yelled out Petty Officer Brown, the baking instructor we had during this class for a week. His usual manner of talking involved the non-creative use of profanity.

"I did," I said as we were all finishing wiping down the equipment.

"Do you realize what you just did?" He said with his already red face getting even redder. "You stupid -----, who told you to fill these bins?"

I didn't know what I did wrong or why he was so mad and everybody stopped fully what they were doing to watch me get my butt chewed out and probably made to walk the plank.

"Nobody told me to fill them MS1," I answered, still trying to figure out what I could have done to make him so mad at me.

"All of these flours are different, you stupid ----. I can't believe what you just did to me. Now I have to throw all the flour away cause you stupid ---- mixed up the flours."

Petty Officer Brown was now in a complete rage and I was getting the chewing out of a lifetime for something I didn't see as a big deal.

"Oh, are you thinking I mixed up the flour?" I said as I started to pull the bins out from under the table. "I didn't. Look."

I proceeded to lift the plastic lids off the bins and put my hands into the flour.

"This flour," I said, "is a high-gluten flour. You can tell by the color and the weight the flour has in your hands." I moved onto the next bin in the same manner. "This is a pastry flour that is bleached. See how white it is?" I continued on from bin to bin, showing him how the label on the bin matched up with the product I put into them until we went through every bin.

Petty Officer Brown stood there and asked, "How do you know all this about flour?"

I went on to tell him what I used to do and tried my best to prove that I was not the simple-minded numbskull he thought I was. The rest of the class just stood there staring at me as if I just cost them our grades for this class.

"Let me see your products and what you made tonight," he said.

After showing him everything we made that night and upon his satisfaction all he said next was, "You had me scared there for a minute. OK wrap it up and get the ---- out of here."

That's it, I thought, no apology?

It's never easy to get your butt chewed but even worse if you get it chewed for no reason. I was dreading going back to class the next night for fear of more of this treatment but did my best to shake it off and not let it affect my performance. My goal was to finish the course with flying colors and right then I wondered if I'd even finish at all.

As I walked into class that next night I could feel all eyes were on me and nobody was pleased with me. Even though I proved I didn't do anything wrong, that didn't seem to matter. I was doomed.

"Macfarlane," Petty Officer Brown said as we were gathered standing around the work bench awaiting our assignments for the night. "I have got some paperwork to do tonight so you're in charge of the class and don't ---- it up."

"Was this how he was apologizing to me?" I thought. It still bugged me that he didn't say he was sorry. I didn't want to take charge. I wanted a public apology to regain what little self dignity I had.

"Yes, Petty Officer Brown," I said as he handed me the list of products to make that night.

We had a pretty easy list and were finished about an hour and a half early. I supervised the mixing and baking of everything and even spent the last 45 minutes washing pots and pans in the deep three compartment sink that is set up to wash, rinse and sanitize. I was trying to do something else other than fill the bins for fear of actually making a mistake this time and wrecking what I saw as a really good night.

I went into Petty Officer Brown's office and let him know we were finished and handed him back our production list with the amounts of product prepared for each item that night. He looked it over and said thanks and followed me back into the kitchen where everybody was standing around in hopes to get out early since we were done.

After a brief inspection of the food and cleanliness of the kitchen he opened up a discussion by asking if anybody had any questions or comments on baking. Nobody did. You could tell everybody was just ready to get out of there. After an awkward few seconds he gave us permission to leave. I kind of felt sorry for him that nobody wanted to talk so, as I was leaving, I peaked into his office and asked if he could put donuts on the menu tomorrow because I would like to make some.

We ended up spending an hour just talking about life in general and hanging out. I enjoyed it and we seemed to get along well after he opened up. He was a submariner and was telling me what a great time he had in Scotland and that I should try and go to submariner school after this school to get stationed on a submarine.

In Holy Loch, Scotland, the US Navy had a submarine base that was the main stopping point for all submarines stationed in the North Atlantic. At the time, the North Atlantic was a real hotspot during the Cold War with the Soviet Union and probably the busiest sea lanes for cat and mouse games with the Russians.

I didn't join the Navy to go back to Scotland though but did consider going to submariner school. I joined to learn how to cook and hopefully see some parts of the world that I normally would never consider.

In boot camp, when we would hear about ports from our experienced instructors, all of the senior sailors would agree that WESTPAC's (western Pacific cruises) were the best duty you could ever experience on board a ship with warm weather continuously, and Australia and Hawaii being the favorite ports. That's exactly what I was looking for, adventure and seeing the places of the world you only dream about seeing.

I took Petty Officer Brown's advice and applied to go to Submarine Training School in Groton, Connecticut, for when I would graduate from culinary training. I was turned down due to not being a US citizen. Apparently that was a requirement for whatever reason. I don't know why but there was nothing I could do about it. I had not thought about gaining citizenship before, so I looked at this as something I would try to achieve later on. I would just wait and see where I would end up after school and see where the Navy would take me.

Towards the end of school, we all had the chance to fill out a dream sheet for choices on which duty stations we would like to go to after school. The reason they call it a dream sheet is that, rumor had it, you would be dreaming to even think you had a choice of which ship to go to.

Despite the rumors, I put in for three ships. One was the USS Carl Vinson. A brand new aircraft carrier that was due to take a cruise around the world. Something I was very keen to do. The other two were re-commissioned battleships from the World War II era, the USS New Jersey and the USS Wisconsin.

I was dreaming apparently. I didn't get any ships. Instead I was told that I didn't receive any orders yet and would have to wait for orders. A week later I was told that I would be getting stationed overseas and I needed to complete overseas screening in order to receive my orders. I still had no clue where overseas I was going, so happily started the process I was assigned to complete and upon satisfactory results get my orders.

All in all it took about three more weeks. I was going to work as part of an Admiral's staff in Naples, Italy. When I got this news I couldn't believe my luck. It was like finding a golden ticket in a Willy Wonka bar. All the hard work I did in school had paid off and as a result of finishing top in my class I was given the chance to demonstrate my abilities to one of the highest ranking officers in the Navy. A four-star Admiral.

I had no idea what to expect or what I would be doing. But I was more enthusiastic about going to Italy than I was about going to work, to be honest, so I went straight to the book store to buy a couple of those travel companion books that tourists use with all the places of interest about your destination as well as what turned out to be a very handy glossary of English - Italian translations.

However disappointed I was about not going to a ship, I made the best of the situation. I wondered what shipboard life would have been like since, for the past four months, I was training to be on a ship. Well, that day would come, I was sure of it and eventually it did.

After leaving San Diego, I headed back to New Jersey on leave, after which I was scheduled to fly to Naples, Italy, from Philadelphia, with stops in the Azores and Spain along the way.

Of course I paid a visit to Chris, my recruiter, after I got home. He was happy to hear about how well I did in school then filled me in on how much Naples was a dirty port city that is riddled with crime and stores that are notorious for ripping off the American sailors. I kidded that it was just like Kearny and Newark then and I should feel right at home. We laughed for an hour or so about it and how I felt about boot camp and my naval experiences so far.

Chris was a good guy and I thanked him for helping with the enlistment process and making me comfortable with the whole transition. It's not easy going from a life where I was pretty independent and self sufficient to a life where you're told what to do and what time to do it.

I was anxious to leave after making my rounds in Kearny and see the guys back at the bakery. I went to New York City a few times. Joe, Ron's son, took me to Little Italy to celebrate my new experience. That was incredibly nice of him to do. I went camping for a few days in Saranac Lake, New York, and visited my Uncle Tommy and Willie also.

I cooked a bunch at home and studied my Navy courses that I had to complete for my first promotion to Seaman Apprentice which I was eligible for in four months.

The temptation to fly to Scotland for a week was great but Mum thought it best for me to save my money so I could head home to Scotland from Italy after I got settled in and that is exactly what I did.

After getting to Kearny, I ate like a king. Meat pies, fish and chips and everything else I missed. I guess I was making up for the lack of food in California. I have never cared for Mexican food and it seemed like that was all that there was available to eat.

# I AM RIGHT WHERE I WANT TO BE

Upon my arrival in Naples the first thing I noticed was how awful the air smelled. There is a massive volcano there, overlooking the whole bay, called Mt. Vesuvius. This was the first volcano that I had ever seen and I was unaware that with the picturesque beauty of a volcano also comes the dreadful smell of the sulfur that lurks beneath. The smell was pretty strong but it didn't take long for me to get used to. Besides, it didn't smell as bad as our first apartment in New Jersey and like it or not, this was going to be home for the next two years.

The second thing I noticed was how crazy the Italians were on the road. It was pretty scary and I thought there was no way I would be able to drive here without ending up in a hospital. Little Fiat Cinquecento's scooting around, dodging mopeds and scooters everywhere, turning three lanes of traffic into five as if that was normal. Think of taking everything you learn in a driver's manual and throw it out the window. This was sheer madness. Red lights meant proceed with caution at your own risk and green lights meant the same thing since the cross road had the red and they were going to go through it should there be an opening.

The scenery was beautiful, I thought, with steep green hills cut to look like stairs and rustic old sandstone houses. It felt great to be back in Europe. The barracks were in an old hotel that sat on a cliff overlooking the Mediterranean, with a spectacular view of the islands of Ischia and Capri, in a town called Pozzuoli. The world-famous Flavian Amphitheater was right down the road. Pozzuoli is also where Saint Paul first landed in Italy on his pilgrimage to Rome. There is also the church of San Gennaro, the patron saint of Naples, in Pozzuoli which was said to contain the blood of the saint that changes from a solid to a liquid twice a year. If it didn't liquefy, the Neapolitans felt there would be bad luck in the city.

I was only there a day and was already falling in love with the place. I reported to work the next day at the NATO base just down the hill from where I was living. The building was impressive. Marble everywhere, with two floors of offices in a U-shape. The kitchen where I would be working was on the south side of the second floor and contained its own dining room and bar. There was a six point burner, convection oven and wooden workbench just like we had at the bakery. I thought of Shep as I checked for cigarette burns along the edge. There were none.

I was one of two new guys who came straight from boot camp. Rodney was the other sailor and he was from someplace in Ohio.

The kitchen had a whole division of people working there. It was led by Lieutenant Cottrell and Senior Chief Peralta. Chief Inocencio was my immediate boss and we ended up becoming great friends during my time in Naples. He was a great guy that spent most of his career in Italy. He married an Italian and spoke Italian fluently. The rest of the sailors there were all second class petty officers. That meant I would have little time cooking and lots of time doing dishes. I was right. Rodney and I were the grunts doing the shopping and the dishes every day. Ironing the linens and shining the silver while dressing up in an old-school waiter's jacket and bow tie to deliver coffee to the Admiral.

The Admiral was James B. Busey. I was scared to death to meet him at first but I ended up having a great time working for him. It was said that he used to fly crop dusters in Indiana as a teenager before joining the Navy as a pilot. He was also said to have been good friends with then Vice President George HW Bush.

On my first day at the office, I was told that we didn't just work at the office. We also had to spend duty nights at the Admiral's house which was called Villa Nike. It was in the Posillipo section of Naples, about a 30 minute drive from the base.

The Admiral also had a barge, a 52 foot Chris Craft yacht, along with a P-3 Orion turboprop airplane. Our duties would involve supporting the Admiral in all capacities.

This sounded to me that it was going to be a great tour.

That day, I asked if I could go with the duty person to Villa Nike to learn the duties there. Senior Chief Peralta asked me if I was sure, since I just got there.

"Absolutely Senior Chief," I said without hesitation. I wanted to learn as much as I could, as quick as I could, and demonstrate that I had initiative.

Senior Chief gave me the glance over and said that it was fine if I went.

At first glance of the Villa, I was astonished at how hidden it was from the street. There was a guard shack with armed Carabinieri at the gate and they would come out and check the car over for explosives and check our IDs. The Carabinieri were in charge of the Admiral's safety and were also his drivers in a bullet proof Alpha Romeo that stopped at nothing while driving.

There were two chief petty officers who were stationed in the Villa full time, Chief Reyes and Chief Mendoza. They seemed like good guys at first and turned out to be great friends to me throughout my tour. Both loved to cook and they were both always joking around in the kitchen. It was hard to tell when they were serious sometimes but later I found out they were never serious. I had a great time working with them both.

Villa Nike was an old mansion with about 28 rooms, built in the late 1700s. It was a show piece and the most beautiful house I had ever seen. Everything about it was elegant, from the brass carpet railings on the spiral staircase to the gold leaf table in the foyer. The ceilings were about 18 feet tall. There were two guest rooms downstairs next to the parlor, a guest bathroom with a sitting room that was about the size of my Mum's apartment, two social rooms, a dining room and a pantry next to the kitchen that was filled with crystal glasses and gold rimmed plates.

The kitchen was also beautiful with an eight foot marble table in the center of the room. It had three stoves, two refrigerators, a broiler and just about everything you needed to crank out some serious food.

Our office was across the hall and had a desk and a bed. That's it. The basement housed the real workings of the house with a laundry room, the chief's office and a spare bedroom where I would be spending the night. There was a walk-in wine cooler and a break room that you could have a football game in.

We didn't have to prepare dinner that evening since the Admiral and his wife Jean were out at a function and wouldn't arrive home until around ten or so.

We would get buzzed from the guard shack when the Admiral would arrive at the gate letting us know he was on his way and allowing us time to get our jackets on and greet him at the door. As the Admiral came into the house with his wife he greeted me with a big smile and shook my hand. Dave, the other sailor, introduced us and told him this was my first day in country. He was impressed by me being there so fast and that was exactly the impression I was looking to have. If Ron taught me one thing it was to always make a good first impression and do it with a firm handshake. Thanks Ron.

Over the course of that week, I made my rounds checking in to all the offices that were required to know you made it on station and most importantly so they could pay you. In the course of the check in process, I was notified that I could not get the security clearance necessary to work there and they would have to sort things out with Washington. I couldn't believe it. It turned out because I was not a citizen, I wasn't supposed to be assigned to a base where I would need a secret clearance and somehow somebody had missed that in San Diego.

In the meantime, I would have to sign in as a guest each day until the matter was resolved since I couldn't get a security badge. I ended up doing this for months without complaining. I didn't want to leave, I liked it there.

The Admiral had an aide called Captain Stephen "Tim" Quigley. He also was a Navy pilot and was extremely cordial when we met. He was an older gentleman with frosty grey hair dressed in his perfectly pressed winter blue uniform. This guy always looked sharp and was a true hard working professional, which later became noticeable by the hours he worked to keep the Admiral on time and on track. He never sat at his desk to work. He chose to stand at a large podium as if commanding a large audience at a lecture but instead he would face the wall with the Admiral's daily schedule front and center at precisely eye level. He never had even a hair out of place and always conducted himself in the most professional manner. He had a wife and three small children and used to fly the P-3 Orion out of Alaska. Captain Quigley was a Naval Academy graduate from Annapolis. He wore his wedding band on his ring finger along with his academy class ring.

Most 'Ring-knockers' wore their rings in this fashion signifying that they were married to both the Navy and their wives. Committed to both, without preference of one over the other. But, of course, the Navy has no room for competition and is very jealous of any distraction from the mission. That is why Navy wives DO have the toughest job in the Navy.

I got to know Captain Quigley quite well. After work on Saturdays, if I had office duty, we would go to the gym and play squash together. He was incredibly competitive but patient with me mishitting the ball a lot. I still keep in touch with him today.

I volunteered to work as much as possible at my new duty station. I figured what better way than to spend my time than to work? I couldn't go out much since I didn't have a car and I didn't speak Italian yet. So I wanted to work.

The Admiral's barge was called the Grazie Due, which means Thank You Two. The boat was seized from drug runners back in the 1970s and given to the Admiral's post as Commander in Chief Naval Forces Southern Europe. It was commanded by Master Chief Boatswains Mate Steve Shuler. Master Chief Shuler had salt water running through his veins instead of blood and was every bit the poster child for what you'd imagine a career enlisted sailor with 32 years in the Navy would look like.

He was a tall, good looking guy with slicked back black hair and a pencil mustache similar to Clark Gable. He wore long sideburns that the old-school sailors would traditionally wear since having them as far down as the very bottom of your ear lobe was as far as you were allowed and the closest you could have to a beard. One of his favorite lines to use on new guys like me was, "Where are you from?" He would ask this as if wanting to know you better.

"Scotland," I said as if he should have known.

"What's your Mom's name?" he would continue

"Catherine," I replied

"Hmm, Catherine?" he would say while looking down and rubbing his chin as if thinking of what next to say.

"How old are you?" was his next question and by now whoever he was pulling this on, including me, would think were about to become drinking buddies and he's just trying to get to know me better.

"Nineteen," I said as if that was old enough to go drinking with him.

"Scotland. Hmmm. Catherine. Hmmm. That would be around 1967-68 am I right?" he would continue and he was a whiz at doing math in his head real fast, come to find out.

"Yes, Master Chief that is right," I replied

"Well, I can't say for sure," he said, starting to grin. "But I was known to have pulled into Scotland around that time off a long cruise but I don't remember her name." And then lay into a long and hearty laugh as if to assume he's my Dad. No matter how many times I would later hear him say this, I would always bust out laughing as if it was the first time. I am even laughing right now while writing this.

Master Chief had tattoos over most of his body. Spider webs on each elbow with hinges tattooed on the creases between the forearm and biceps. Sea horses on each forearm and a letter on each finger that made no sense until he interlocked his fingers to reveal his favorite profanity. He had every port he visited on a Western Pacific tour tattooed on his right calf. Boat propellers (screws) on each butt cheek with a caption reading "KEEP CLEAR" and a port and starboard light on each shoulder blade.

Master Chief and I hit it off right from the beginning. I volunteered to cook on his boat for the Admiral whenever needed and soon became the permanent cook on board. This meant working every Saturday that I did not have office duty and Sundays if the Admiral decided to skip church and go for a cruise. We would cruise around Capri mostly and slip down the Almalfi coast. Master Chief was an expert coxswain and loved what he did for a living.

Master Chief Shuler was also an intellectual guy with a wealth of knowledge. Not just about the sea but about everything. He held his own pilot's license, something we had in common, and he was great to talk with. Whenever I was on board the barge, I would prep the meals for the Admiral and his guests in the small galley on board, then make up a quick lunch for the crew. On my first trip out I got so sea sick from standing in the small space and trying to cook that Master Chief let me take breaks topside to get some fresh air. He let me know, after we got back to Nisida to drop the Admiral off, that I wasn't allowed back on his boat unless I promised to get my sea legs. Then laughed with the deep bass laugh that was so loud it fit his personality perfectly. I politely told him thanks for the warning and I'll see him next weekend.

Back on base, I tried to pick up what I could in the kitchen from both Neil and Chris. They made the daily lunches for the Admiral and his staff as well as catered to any guests we had in the dining room. The first smell I remember from my first day washing dishes was onions and peppers being sautéed in a cast iron skillet with garlic and olive oil. I instantly fell in love. I had never smelled a food so pleasing before and having never tried peppers before, I couldn't wait to see what went with the peppers. It was a stuffed airline breast of chicken (airline meaning it had the wing bone in it) with a blend of Italian soft cheeses and served with turned potato fondant.

I would always rush to get the dishes done so I could see how everything was prepared and help if needed. Chris was always more eager to show me how to cook than Neil although Neil was the better cook of the two having been a graduate of the Culinary Institute of America, the school I couldn't afford to go to.

Chris was also the main cook aboard the Admiral's plane. He seemed to travel quite a lot and whenever he would come back from England, where the Admiral also had an office, he would bring me back the English newspapers for me to catch up on things at home.

It wasn't long before I started becoming accustomed to the Italian language and, most of all, the food. The Italians really know how to enjoy food. I loved getting my cappuccino in the morning before work and enjoying a coronetto or graffa. The Italians taught me how to be passionate about food and stripped me of my phobias, except for mashed potatoes, and I became more adventurous in my eating habits.

Chief Inocencio introduced me to the Carabinieri dining hall and man was it ever good. I had never had food like that before in my life. Everything was done so perfectly that you would have thought the kitchen was packed with world class chefs, but it wasn't. It was staffed by older Italian ladies who did a magnificent job. There was also wine on the tables to enjoy. I must admit that I was a little buzzed heading back to the office and I couldn't wait to go back.

I never thought pasta could be so good when only tossed in olive oil, fresh garlic and basil. I had slices of tomatoes, that were the most perfect tomatoes I had ever seen, with sliced buffalo mozzarella and more basil and oil. Slices of cantaloupe melon were also enjoyed with prosciutto ham, some sea salt and escarole lettuce with what tasted like lemon juice and vinegar.

Everything was so fresh I could hardly believe it. I wish I could have eaten there everyday but, as a cook, I kind of had to work during lunch. Every chance I got I went back, though not enough.

I thought, as a kid, that I had the passion to be a chef but never really realized what true passion for food was until I was in Italy. Food is such a big part of everybody's lives and I began to realize what I thought was passion was simply a desire to be passionate about food.

At about three months into my tour I was working in the office, the villa and the barge. I was also working six days a week guaranteed and loving it. On the Admiral's next trip to London I decided to fly up to England before him, spend a few days with my family then meet him in London and fly on his plane back to Naples.

I was long overdue to go home and couldn't wait to see everybody there. I was especially looking forward to seeing my younger sister Joanne, who was there with my cousin Catherine.

Over the course of my first year in Italy I had been really enjoying not just the people but the whole Italian experience. I grew to love the place and drive just as crazy as the rest of them.

This reminds me of a funny story of when I was back in New Jersey visiting from Italy, and I had to drive my Mum to work in order to use her car for the day. I was driving down the road and all of a sudden the car in front of me stopped. I had no idea why he stopped so I squeezed around him, looked at him like he was crazy and proceeded to speed up away from him. After a second, I finally realized why he stopped. It was for a red light. After confirming this in my mirror, I ducked down a side street and proceeded with extreme caution. I was lucky on that one.

As I started to get to know the Admiral and his wife from my time at the villa, I became more comfortable and confident in my work there. The work was hard yet enjoyable while serving a ton of parties there. It was a tradition to serve French style with a platter on one arm and serving utensils in the other hand. Everything we did we did with pride. The food was always perfect thanks to Chief's Reyes and Mendoza.

I started to get to know the other Admirals that worked various posts for the Navy and one in particular was always glad to see me. He was Vice Admiral Kendall Moranville. Admiral Moranville was, at the time, the commander of the sixth fleet. He would always take an interest in me the same way Admiral Busey did. He would ask how I liked Italy, what brought me to join the Navy and how I liked the Navy so far.

I would go on to serve Admiral Moranville many times. He was a real salty sailor and loved the Navy. It was rumored that he kept a loaded pistol in an ankle holster on his leg. He too was a naval pilot. In the post he held in Gaeta, Italy, he had a ship that cruised him around the Mediterranean. The ship was an older amphibian ship and he had the Navy give him a guided missile cruiser to ride on because it was more of a war ship.

Admiral Moranville was a great guy and his last words to me were, "Anything I can ever do for you, you let me know."

The crew I worked with in Italy was the best crew I worked with in my entire Navy career because there was such a unique sense of professionalism and authentic respect for each other that was never undermined by petty drama or trying to outshine the other for personal gain.

We would spend a lot of time with the Admirals and their families in both professional and personal settings. Learning how to balance this while maintaining professionalism was always easier when having such a great crew to support you.

Mrs. Busey and I would spend time picking tomatoes in the back yard or walking down the street to the vegetable stands, not so much for the produce but for the conversation. They are very much regular people too and she was a great person to get to know.

In the ten years I spent in the Navy, I worked for two Admirals, Admiral Busey in Italy and another four-star in Pearl Harbor, Hawaii.

Both Admirals were great guys to work for and both Admirals had great families to work for also. The Chief I worked for in Hawaii though didn't like me interacting with the Admiral nor his wife and kids. For some odd reason he and I did not get along. One day, while the Admiral and his wife were on a trip away from Hawaii, he started complaining that he isn't here to clean up after the kids and who do they think they are making a mess and expecting us to clean it up. I told him to chill and that was our job so let it go. He didn't like that so he started giving me a hard time, and then went down to the Admiral's office to complain. When the Admiral got back with his wife he was clearly upset. His wife pulled us in the kitchen and was disappointed that one of us went to the office to complain about their kids.

The Chief blamed me for it and after that the Admiral never spoke to me again. To this day, I regret not telling them who did it but since he was my Chief I just couldn't do it.

When I first got to the base in Hawaii, I noticed that there wasn't a dining hall on base and stopped in to see the base commander to find out why there wasn't a mess on the base. He didn't know why there wasn't and told me that if I could find out how to get one that he would support me. A year later, and after working evenings to write letters and allocate billets and equipment, I had a galley on that base and did so as a Petty Officer Second Class. My Chief refused to recognize me for doing so and would not put it in my annual evaluation. Upon my departure from the Navy, he took credit for creating the mess hall himself and was rewarded with a nice promotion.

The reason I told you the story about the situation in Hawaii was not because of bad feelings for what happened but to illustrate and emphasize how special all the people I worked with in Italy are to me. Out of all the duty stations I was stationed in, Italy remained the first and the best.

Back in Naples, Chris was getting out of the Navy to pursue being a missionary for his church. Chris was Polish-American and felt a calling to minister to the Polish while they were under Soviet rule. Our staff needed a volunteer to take his place cooking on the plane. Of course, I was the first to raise my hand. I got the job.

I would be the junior cook on board as a Seaman and answered to the First Class who stayed with the squadron in Sigonella, Sicily.

We would fly all over Europe as well as quarterly trips back to the US for the Admirals' conferences held at the Pentagon.

The head enlisted man on the plane was Senior Chief Shellenberger and he was a lot like Master Chief Shuler, as in being a career sailor and loving everything about the Navy. He always looked his best and was very squared away. He was a career Aviation Boatswains Mate and was the utility guy that got things done for the crew. Senior Chief was the go-to guy for whatever you needed anywhere in the world. He showed me all the things to look for in the safety and well being of the aircraft. He didn't know that I had already been to flight school as a kid and knew as much about planes as he did. I didn't want to seem as a know-it-all so I must admit I downplayed what I knew so he would walk me through what to do and what not to do. I respected him a great deal and didn't want to bring any unnecessary friction between us. I was just a cook and liked keeping it that way.

Senior Chief (Shelly, he went by) would call everybody Squid. Squid is a term to refer to a sailor and is usually a derogatory term when used by someone outside of the Navy.

"Welcome aboard Squid," was the greeting I got from Senior Chief. Then he introduced me to the crew and took me to meet the planes commander, Lt. Commander Christopher Jameson.

"Squid," Senior Chief said in the crusty voice that made him sound hard and as if he was a seaman who served under John Paul Jones. "This is Commander Jameson. The best ---- pilot the Navy could muster. He can land this plane on a stick of butter in the middle of a hurricane, so be respectful to him."

Of course I would, I thought. LCDR Jameson was a great pilot and loved playing jokes on the VIP visitors that would sit in the cockpit behind him during take off and landings. He did things like walk on board the plane moving his hands around his pockets and asking if anybody has seen the keys since it was time to go and he can't find the keys. His favorite would be to tap the gauges as if something was wrong and look at the co-pilot with a face of concern. Whoever was sitting behind him, depending on how comfortable flyers they were, would get up and head to the back with a sense of fear in their face hoping that if they leave the cockpit everything would be alright. Funny stuff.

One time we flew into Berlin. This was when the Berlin Wall was still up and Master Chief Shuler came with us for the ride and to check out Berlin. The Admiral was going to stay there and we were flying home without him only to go back a week later to pick him up. Apparently some genius thought the Navy would save money on our hotel if we dropped him off and flew home. This of course added two more flights to the trip and the fuel costs were way more than our hotel would be for the month. This thinking didn't last long by the way.

Anyway, on the way home from Berlin LCDR Jameson let Master Chief Shuler fly the plane since we had no passengers on board. I had never seen a guy so happy. Master Chief had only flown single engine aircraft before and here he was at the controls of a four engine plane at twenty seven thousand feet. He looked like a kid at Christmas. I wish I had a camera. I wanted to frame that smile.

For weeks after he would always tell the story of flying the P-3 with such excitement and say, "How did I do Dave? Did I do good?" whenever he saw me.

"You did great Master Chief," I would always say. Even if we were headed for the Alps I would still tell him the same thing. I would never have wrecked that moment for him and he really did do a great job.

Being an avid football fan, I loved going to the Napoli games. Mario, who owned a pizza shop near where I lived in Pozzuoli, would go with me on occasion. He was born in Italy and lived in New Jersey as a young man but preferred to return home rather than stay in America. We had a lot in common but most of all we loved being able to go to the stadium among thousands of like-minded Neapolitans going crazy to cheer on their home team which was fronted by one of the most famous football players next to Pele, Diego Maradonna.

On the few occasions I had time off, I would travel around Italy soaking up as much of the culture as I could. I started driving as crazy as they did. I started eating as much as they did and I was a lot more comfortable with speaking to Italians and not letting a language barrier stop me from living. Unfortunately, too many Americans that were stationed there would only frequent the American bases and their amenities. They wouldn't learn the language nor experience the culture. This to me was a sin. How could you not want to share in everything this beautiful country had to offer? It was very hard for me to leave Italy when I did, but the Admiral and his aides thought it best if I did what every sailor needs to do. Go to sea.

Before I left Italy I had one more piece of business to attend to and that was to get my high school diploma. Lt. Dennis Yeatman, my new division officer, made an appointment for me to take the test. He gave me two days off to complete it and wasn't going to accept a failing grade. If it wasn't for him, I don't think I would have even bothered with it. I am glad I did.

Upon passing all my tests I was now a high school graduate.

## THE GREATEST GIFT EVER

This chapter is dedicated to a man that gave me the greatest gift ever. Admiral James B. Busey.

Hopefully you remember me saying how I had to sign in as a visitor each day to go to work since I couldn't get a badge that indicated that I had a secret clearance.

It was early October 1987 and Captain Quigley called me down to his office.

"We are flying to DC in a couple weeks," he said, as he shuffled some papers atop his podium. "The Admiral wants you on board for this trip so get your crap together and be ready to come with us, OK?"

"Yes sir," I said, and was wondering why the Admiral wanted me to go on this trip. I hadn't started working on the plane yet but, "maybe he needs me to work in DC," I thought as I headed back to the kitchen and stopping in the office to give Senior Chief Peralta the heads up to what was just said.

The day came when I was flying out and still didn't have a clue why I was on board. I was just a passenger. It was a 13 hour flight to get to Andrews Air Force Base outside Washington DC. As we were getting close to landing, the Admiral handed me an envelope and said, "While we are here in DC, I want you to take this letter to the immigration services in Newark and ask to see the person in charge. Once you get that person, hand this envelope to them and then do as you're told."

"Yes sir," I replied and glanced over the plain white envelope inspecting both sides as if to get a clue what this was about.

I did like the Admiral said and caught a flight up to Newark, and headed to my Mum's apartment since it was too late to head to immigration that afternoon. I went the next morning, very early, to beat the line and wore my dress blues so I could skip the line and head straight up to the office as directed.

Once upstairs, I proceeded to the window that prevented anybody from having physical contact with the receptionist and politely asked for the person in charge in regards to an urgent matter.

She looked at me puzzled, of course, probably wondering what a sailor would want with the person in charge of immigration. She then proceeded to make a phone call.

A few minutes later an elderly African-American lady came out from a solid metal door and asked what she could help me with. I handed her the envelope and said nothing.

She opened the envelope and looked up from behind her bi-focal glasses towards me. She then proceeded to read the contents of the letter.

I still had no idea what the letter said or what the contents were within that white envelope, but from the expression on her face I could tell it was serious. After reading she removed her glasses and thought for a second, then said, "Follow me."

After being escorted to a desk, I was told to take a seat and wait while the lady whom read the letter asked to talk to the lady, whose desk I was at, in private. I had no idea what was going on and just sat there wondering what to expect.

Turns out, after the lady came back to her desk, she was instructed to process me for naturalization and I would have to complete an application process and answer a few questions. Throughout the whole process I was treated like a VIP. I never had to fill out any paperwork myself and only had to sign my application.

The process took about two hours and then I was given instructions to get my picture taken downstairs then be in the courthouse to be sworn in that day.

I couldn't believe it. I was totally blown away with what the Admiral had done for me. It was the greatest gift I had ever received and showed how much the Admiral thought of me.

When standing in line for my photo, a lady that was in front of me turned around to talk to me, probably since I was in my dress blues.

"What are you doing here?" she said as if she knew me.

"I'm here to get my picture taken for my citizenship," I replied.

"Where are you from?" she then asked.

"I'm from Scotland," I said as if she should already know that because of my name tag and bright red hair. Definitely an assumption on my part.

"Where is that?" she then said.

I couldn't believe what I just heard. Where is that? Are you kidding me? That was a first for me and I was so surprised to hear that question that for once I didn't have a smart alec answer for her. I just shook my head and thanked God she was up before I could answer.

At 4:30 on the afternoon of October 31, I was sworn in with about 80 other newly-initiated citizens. It was quite an emotional ceremony for the vast amounts of nationalities that all now had one thing in common. We were all citizens of the United States.

A few days later, I was back in DC and on board the P-3 waiting for the Admiral to arrive. Once he came up the ladder I stood just off to the side and greeted him as he came through to the cabin.

"Well? Did you do as I asked?" he said with a big grin.

"Sir, I don't know how to thank you," I said as I pulled my naturalization certificate out of an envelope to show him the evidence that I did exactly as he asked. "Thank you so much," I said as I reached out for his hand to show my appreciation.

"You're welcome, Dave," he said, while shaking my hand and looking over the certificate. "Now you're one of us, congratulations."

I couldn't believe what he did for me and couldn't think of a way to truly show my gratitude without just saying thank you.

Everybody, back at the office, speculated that the Admiral had George Bush write the letter to make it happen but I had absolutely no idea and failed to ask for the letter back since it wasn't mine. If it was George Bush maybe that would explain the seriousness of the facial expressions from the lady who helped me. All that mattered to me was going down to the personnel office and getting my security badge, which I had within a few weeks.

There was one last thing that the Admiral did for me that almost made me cry. Every so often the Admiral would convene the staff in his office and host an awards ceremony for anybody that got promoted or would receive special recognition for a job well done.

On this occasion, my Senior Chief told me to get into my dress uniform and be on time for the ceremony. As I was getting changed everybody was telling me that I was getting promoted, giving orders to the South Pole and so on and so on. Basically, busting my chops.

At the ceremony, the Admiral called me next to him and proceeded to tell everybody that I had just become a citizen. He then presented me with a letter of congratulations from Senator Frank Lautenburg from New Jersey and an American flag that was flown above the US Capitol building for me. I was completely blown away and still at a loss for words. This was one of the greatest moments of my naval career thanks to Admiral Busey. He is a true officer and gentleman, and one that I will never forget.

A year and a half later, after I received my orders to the USS Mount Whitney (LCC-20), the Admiral awarded me with a Joint Services Accommodation Medal. What he said next showed me why he did what he did.

"Petty Officer Macfarlane is a hard worker. Whenever I am at the office, at the villa, on board the barge or on board the airplane, Petty Officer Macfarlane has been there working just as hard as he did on his first day here." Remember what I said about first impressions?

I guess I should have told him that working for him and his family for those two years wasn't work. It was my pleasure. But, I'm sure he already knew that.

On the Thanksgiving Thursday, the following month, I volunteered for the villa duty that day so the married guys could be home with their families. Captain Quigley made arrangements with the Admiral to pick me up from the villa, drive to his apartment and spend Thanksgiving dinner with him, his family and friends. I was overwhelmed by their sincere generosity and how much they cared about me. I never thought of myself as special. The acts of selflessness taught me to care about the people around me and this lesson I still practice to this day while expecting nothing in return.

I am sure the Admiral never set out to make me a better person but his actions of leading by example did exactly that.

Thank you, sir.

# GROWING UP AT SEA

After an emotional departure from Italy, I reported for duty on board the USS Mount Whitney (LCC-20), an amphibious command ship out of Norfolk, Virginia, the largest naval base on the Atlantic coast and quite possibly the world. The piers seemed to go on forever littered with every type of ship you could possibly imagine. Aircraft carriers, destroyers, cruisers, frigates, submarines, you name it. It was an endless row of grey and had the hustle and bustle of New York City. There were dungaree-clad sailors everywhere, loading ships and coming and going, all with a sense of urgency.

It was quite an impressive skyline. Antennas filled the skyline and the cabby, a retired squid, was kind enough to give me a tour of the base before dropping me off at Pier 25.

Once on board, I managed to wrestle all my bags down the narrow passageways and ladders to the supply berthing where I would be living for the next three years.

Being a Third Class by this time, I thought that I would at least get a decent rack to sleep in but boy was I wrong. I ended up on a top rack in a compartment of 62 racks, stacked three high. The top racks were the worst since they didn't contain a compartment underneath to stow your belongings so I had to find two extra lockers to put my gear into. There was hardly any room on the ship at all for my stuff but I did my best to find room.

After getting settled in downstairs and trying to figure out which way was up, I went up the ladder to the next deck where the galley was. The galley is the kitchen. It ran the width of the ship with a serving line on each side where the crew would line up with plastic trays in hand and pick from a variety of meals. There were usually two entrees to pick from, with appropriate sides, as well as cheeseburgers and sandwiches on an express line that you could grab and go if you didn't have time to eat in the dining area.

The galley had a wall of two stacked convection ovens on the forward side and a row of four steam-jacketed kettles on the aft side. The dreaded egg griddle was right next to the port side food line and seeing it brought back my memories from school and how this was going to be a challenge to try and get my groove back without looking like a numbskull in front of the whole crew. It wasn't long before I found out that a cook's reputation would make you or break you with the crew and they all knew who the bad cooks were.

Nobody seemed real friendly that first day and I felt kind of lonely for the first time in ages. I had nobody to show me around so I just laid on my six by four rack and read until I fell asleep that night.

The next day, I just followed the other cooks to the mess decks and wandered around there until I found someone, who looked like they knew what I was supposed to do, in an office next to the galley.

It was my new Chief. He ended up telling me to wait until 6:45 and muster on the mess decks with the rest of the cooks. Once doing so, I got the first chance to see everybody I would be working with. I was one of three white guys and the rest were all African-American. I was surprised by this but it didn't bother me. I knew what it was like to be discriminated against for something beyond my control, my red hair.

I became great friends with a lot of these guys throughout my tour and they loved busting my chops for being the whitest guy they'd ever seen. I would laugh along with them because I must admit, I am pretty white. The red hair didn't help either but once we got to know each other we always had a great time, whether at work or on shore. These guys were my shipmates.

Chief assigned me to work in the Chiefs' Mess. On board a ship this large, the Chiefs had their own dining room and kitchen where there was one supervisor cook and two Third Classes actually doing the cooking on a rotation. I was one of the Third Classes.

I spent six months working in the Chiefs' Mess and it gave me a whole new perspective on the Navy. There was no way I was going to stay in and be like these guys. They were the biggest bunch of whiney babies that I had ever seen. They complained about everything and most of them were a bunch of slobs that never really cared what you thought of them. Just as long as you cleaned up after them.

The only Chief I got along with was Chief Groesbeck. Well technically he was a First Class when we met, then promoted to Chief. He became a very good friend and I got to know him and his wife Helen well. Helen was from Scotland also. Chief Groesbeck met her while stationed in Scotland and we would spend hours talking about home. It felt like home for him also and he went back to live there once he retired from the Navy. He was a hard working, no nonsense sailor, and I got to know him and his crew well. Especially since most of his crew played on the ships soccer team and so did I.

One day, while I was working in the Chiefs' Mess, I heard an Irish voice calling out, "Hey Jimmy, hey Jimmy." I ignored it at first but when it became more persistent I turned around to see who it was and who he was talking to. It turned out he was talking to me. At first I thought he had the wrong guy but once he said, "Are you the Jimmy?" I knew what he was talking about. Jimmy is what you call someone whose name you don't know in Scotland. Similar to Paddy for an Irish guy.

"Aye," I replied while dishing him some Glaswegian banter about calling me Jimmy that made us both laugh. It turned out to one of the greatest friendships that I made and a guy who worked in the electrician shop onboard.

Sean Willis was his name and he was the one who recruited me to play football with the rest of the team. He was born in New York, but raised in Limerick, Ireland. We became great friends and still are to this day. My youngest son, Andrew Sean, is named after him and we spent most of our time together on and off the ship.

After my six months in the Chiefs' Mess and what I regarded as getting paroled, I moved onto the main galley. I was the only white guy working in the galley at the time and I was the guy that got all the crap jobs. Clean the grills, clean the ovens, clean underneath the kettles and, last but not least, I was the eggs-to-order guy.

When I was told to take the griddle and do the eggs I said out loud, "Yes!" I wanted everybody to know this is exactly what I wanted to do and how fortunate I was to have the distinct honor of preparing eggs for my fellow crew. They all looked at me like I was crazy. It was, in fact, the most dreaded job in the galley and nobody, and I mean nobody, liked doing it. Not even me. I just acted excited because

I didn't want the other cooks to think of it that way. I wanted them to think that by doing the eggs you are 'THE MAN' so to say.

It wasn't long before I found my groove. The breakfast line seemed to never end and lasted about an hour and a half. My problem was that I was trying to make every omelet and egg order look like I was serving the Admiral. Perfect. Some of the other cooks got on me for being slow because of this, so my new Chief decided one morning to be my wing man and show me how it's done.

He stood beside me and never touched a thing. All he did was call out to the next guy in line for his order by saying, "Next egg." My job was to have his eggs done by the time he would reach the end of the line. It seemed like Chief would call it out every other second. Even before I could ladle the eggs onto the griddle he would say, "Next egg, next egg, next egg." This went on the whole time and I could tell he was trying to break me. I wasn't going for that. I wanted to break him. I wanted him to lose his voice from yelling "Next egg" as much as he did.

He still never lifted a finger to help. He never took over the situation, only tried to worsen it. But I was determined to win even if it meant this would be the last thing I ever did.

For a brief moment during my hazing I thought of Willie. He would have been my cheerleader next to me saying, "C'mon man, move your rear," although he wouldn't say "rear." "You're too slow. These guys need fed and need fed now. Stop playing with your food and start working. I thought you were from Scotland."

I kept my head down, only stepping back from the griddle every few minutes to wipe the sweat off my brow with a wad of paper towel I kept in my pocket. I'm not sure what anybody else was thinking or doing because I was so focused on the eggs. I was, what they say in the business, in the weeds and couldn't get out.

"Next egg, next egg, next egg," was all I could hear and the orders were flying in. My hand started to cramp from holding the spatula and my omelets were lining up like little soldiers ready for battle in a scene from the revolutionary war. This time, I was the one getting my rear end kicked. I had eggs everywhere it seemed like. All I wanted was for Chief to help rather than try to break me. He never did. Maybe this was his idea of helping, by watching me sink quicker than the Titanic and in front of the whole crew. I could picture it in my head, my burial at sea.

"We have gathered here on the decks of this fine vessel to commit to the sea the worthless cook who couldn't keep up with the egg order and suffered a death from cruel and unusual punishment. We ask for Neptune, God of the Deep, to open up Davy Jones Locker and accept this cook whom we deemed unworthy but gave it his all. Amen."

Chief continued his relentless assault on me with his hands in his pockets the whole time. But I wasn't going to break. I wasn't going to let him win. He used to call me the Admiral's boy and I guess this was his way of showing me up and breaking me down. It didn't work. In the end he could only walk away defeated by my determination and without even saying good job. For the rest of our time together, Chief would call me "Slack," since all the other crew called me 'Mac.' This just showed me how immature he was and I acted as if it never fazed me. But it did.

My arms were killing me after this episode and couldn't wait to swallow what I would guess was a quart of water. I was soaked through to my undershirt and the paper hat I was wearing was barely noticeable. It was soaked right through and hanging onto the back of my head from me pushing it up from wiping my brow so much. I hadn't felt this good since boot camp.

But I must thank Chief for what he did for me that morning. Every guy in that galley that day congratulated me afterwards for what I endured and for never quitting.

I honestly think that they felt sorry for me especially since I never looked at it as a racial thing since it could very easily have been racially looked at by some. I never bothered with any of that crap. I didn't care that I was the only white guy in the kitchen at the time. All I cared about was being a chef and I wasn't going to let this guy bully me into believing I couldn't do it or act as if I never had the ambition to be a chef. So what if I'm the minority, I thought, that won't change how I cook or what I cook.

Chief allowed me to be accepted by the rest of the crew and respected from that day forward. I earned my metal. They would joke with me for days afterwards and Chief never set foot on the egg line with me there ever again and that made me happy.

As for the rest of the crew, they started to realize I was serious about cooking and I didn't look at it as just a job. I did my best to set an example that would show we all cared about feeding the crew the very best way possible. With passion.

Before long they moved me to the bake shop. Nobody knew that I was already a baker and most cooks struggled with this position since everything is more precise than cooking and times and temperature could make for a very bad day if not watched carefully. To me this was the easiest job I could have ever gotten and relished in the fact that I could be as creative as I wanted to be. I made everything I could to show that I knew what I was doing.

It wasn't long before the bakeshop became a mini class on technique and creativity, with me showing anybody who was willing to learn everything from how to roll and proof dough to cake decorating once a month. We ended up making real New York style fruit danish, cheesecakes of all sorts and fresh baked bread that made the Officers' Mess envious. Once the Officers' Mess got wind of what we were doing they started ordering our desserts since the enlisted were eating better than they were and to them it was as if we were committing a sin. I would see officers sneaking down and grabbing donuts off the racks faster than the Mess Cooks could set them out for the crew. We were the envy of the ship and were like celebrities wherever we went.

Our swagger was contagious and everybody in the kitchen, no matter what rank, started taking great care of the foods they were cooking and especially how they presented their works of art to the crew. The days of just throwing it in a pan and serving were over. We went on to be nominated for a feeding award and competed against other ships Navy-wide in recognition of what we were doing. The prestigious Ney award for excellence in food service was coming aboard to inspect our galley. This was a really big deal.

Guys who worked in laundry would wash and press all my uniforms for hooking them up with fresh pastries. The Boatswains

Mates taught me how to braid and tie knots for pastries and let me come out on deck or on the bridge at night as long as I wasn't empty handed.

Now if you are an avid astronomer like I am, and have never been out on the sea on a dark moonless night, then you have missed one of the greatest glories ever. It is like being in space. Everything is quiet and you can see every star in the heavens. It is what I miss most about being at sea. I could stand there for hours until my neck would hurt picking out constellations and staring into the mystery of space. It was as if the sky comes to life at night. You see shooting stars, blinking lights and a Milky Way full of wonder. I had never felt so free.

Cake decorating was one of my specialties. In Italy, I would decorate birthday and wedding cakes for the Americans for extra money that I would use to finance my trips home to Scotland. When the Captain of the ship got wind of what I was doing he started having me decorate cakes for every occasion he could think of. The only downside was I wasn't making any extra money for doing this like I had in Italy, so I turned to cutting hair at five dollars each and tutoring other cooks for the tests we took for promotion.

Around this time is when I met my wife Christina. We got a new cook on board who was this young greenhorn from the sticks in west Michigan, from a town called Greenville. We all felt sorry for how green he was and tried our very best to make him feel comfortable with shipboard life. Our division wasn't the same as when I showed up where people just ignored you. It was as if joining a family and everybody looked out for everybody else. It was exactly the way it was meant to be.

Griswold was his name and after being on board for a few months he needed a ride to meet his girlfriend who was coming down from Greenville to live with him off base. Since he didn't have a car I told him that I would drive him. As we were driving to the place where they were to meet, he told me his girlfriend was coming down with a friend because her Mom didn't want her driving alone. I told him that I didn't care about that and was just dropping him off. After we got to where he was meeting her, he went out to check if she had arrived yet. There was no sign of her. And since this was before cellular phones were popular, he had no idea where she was.

I told him I would wait with him in case she didn't show up so he would have a way back to the ship and he agreed that was a good idea. About five hours, two cups of coffee and three newspapers later, she finally showed up with a beautiful blonde named Christina. After introductions were made and everybody declared how hungry they were, I told Christina to come with me to get some food and let these guys get reacquainted. I gave her a tour of the base and showed her the choices of restaurants to pick from. I then told her that I would show her around Virginia Beach and Norfolk during the next few days before she had to fly home which she agreed to.

After she left for home, we kept in touch by writing to each other until she came back down for the summer to be with Griswold's girlfriend while we went to sea. At that time I asked her if she would date me and she agreed. We had a great time together for a couple of weeks, and then I had to go to sea. I left Christina my car to use while I was gone.

When we got back about six weeks later, we picked up where we left off and spent as much time together as possible. When it was time for Christina to head back to college in Michigan I couldn't stand being apart. We were very much in love with each other and I proposed to her. She said yes. We were engaged! I would fly up to Michigan to see her as much as possible and before long it became too hard to do, so we got married in a very small church in Greenville about a month later and she moved down to Norfolk with me. She is still as beautiful today as the day I met her.

I soon moved off of the ship and we rented a small apartment just off base to start our lives together. Not long after we were married the war broke out in Kuwait and I was back at sea.

During this time I got word that my Dad had died of alcoholism and I left the ship to attend his funeral. It was weird seeing him in the coffin with his new family by his side. I didn't feel loss or sorrow until the next day but I was disappointed in how he chose to live his life. I was hoping there would be a letter or something from him that he would write before dying, confessing his mistakes to me and asking for forgiveness for abandoning his family. There was nothing. No remorse, no apology, no regret.

He was fifty two years old and he owed me more than two hundred and eighty dollars. He owed me a reason for what he did.

We became pregnant the following summer with our first son, David Jr. I was not home when she delivered him. Instead, I was in the North Atlantic during a NATO exercise and about 250 miles north of

Scotland headed to the tip of Norway. The Pastor stationed on board got me into the communications room aboard ship and I got to call Christina just after she delivered David Jr.

I was grateful that he did that for me and I couldn't wait to get home. But it would be six weeks before I would see my wife and son.

Once I received my promotion to Second Class, I was moved up to being the personal cook to the Captain. A job that I wasn't crazy about since the Captain had a reputation for firing his cooks. Unfortunately, I didn't have a say in the matter so I reported for duty to the Captain's cabin which had a small galley next to it and a service window in between to pass the plates to the servers.

When I got up there, I was appalled at the condition the kitchen was in. It was filthy and was being tended to by another cook who was getting out of the Navy and didn't care about anything. All he wanted was to get out and get off this ship.

The Captain had a reputation of being tough and demanding, but I thought that's what Captains were supposed to be. I quickly realized after meeting him that we weren't going to be squash partners any time soon and I wasn't coming over to the house for Thanksgiving. I just had to keep my head down and do what I needed to do to keep him off my back.

I was looking forward to being able to make my own menus for the first time since leaving Italy and tried to think of the dishes we would make for Admiral Busey. I had quite an extensive library of cookbooks, and my school book from Johnson and Wales, but I had the insatiable habit of trying to create my own signature dishes with a few Filipino foods that I learned how to make and try to be as creative and artistic as possible. It was an easy job and I got to know the weather guys that had an office next to my kitchen. It wasn't long before I gave them recipes and they taught me how to forecast weather. Of course after I joked with them on how they forecast the weather.

I missed the mass feeding in the galley downstairs and cooking for the crew. I missed everything about it. Even doing eggs to order. Before I left the galley I was in charge of my own crew and I really missed the guys downstairs and the fun we had even though we worked our tails off day and night.

The Captain was up for rotation and his replacement was soon to take over. Captain David L. Brewer III. The new Captain was great to work for and actually talked to me like a human being. Turned out he talked to everybody like they were human beings and turned out to be a great Captain.

Captain Brewer went on to become an Admiral and we still keep in touch to this day also.

The new responsibilities of being a husband and a father forced me to re-enlist for another five years. I waited until the last possible minute to do so until all efforts for a job were exhausted and I couldn't take the risk of being unemployed with a wife and son.

I was due for shore duty soon after my tour on the ship and was considering going back to Europe. I remembered that the Admiral's office in London had cooks and thought I would give that a try and see what was available. Even though it wasn't Scotland, I wanted Christina to experience Britain and what it was like where I came

147

from. She had never been outside of the country before and going to Norfolk was the furthest she had ever been.

In the Navy we had detailers which were like HR people and managed job openings around the world. When I called my detailer, whom handled cooks, the closest I could get to Europe was Iceland. I didn't want that so I passed and even tried going back to Italy. The place I loved. Nothing open. I couldn't get the Far East either due to expense and the only thing they offered me was staying in Norfolk. Neither of us wanted to stay in Norfolk, but I remembered that Admiral's cooks have their own detailer and I thought I would give that a try since I had experience.

After about a hundred phone calls to the detailer, it was impossible to get through since the phone was always busy, I finally got through. I introduced myself and told her a little about me and my experience and asked if London was available. She was quick to say no but, "How would you like to work for the Vice President of the United States in Washington, DC?"

## WASHINGTON BOUND

After inquiring if the detailer was sure she had the right person on the other end of the phone, I took a leap of faith and said, "Yes, I would like to work for the Vice President."

She proceeded to tell me that I would receive orders to report to the Navy Annex in Washington DC to begin the interview process which would take two to three days. The very next day the Master Chief in charge of officer feeding, my boss, called me into the office.

"What the ---- is this ----, Macfarlane?" he asked, with his normal use of Navy metaphors and handed me a sheet of paper that had more dots and dashes than words. For some reason the Navy loved doing that. They hated empty space in a letter and filled it up with dots and dashes to make it look more official. I think whoever is in charge of communications for the Navy has a brother in the ink ribbon business.

"Looks like my orders, Master Chief," I said smiling and waving it in the air like a winning ticket from a horse race I bet heavily on.

Master Chief used to work at the Navy Annex in Washington so he was real curious as to what I was up to. You see, me and old Master Chief did not get along. I kicked him out of my kitchen once for not wearing a hat and he never forgot that day. He was absolutely nothing like any of the other Master Chiefs I ever worked with.

Truth is, I didn't respect him. He didn't know how to cook. He was in the Navy for 28 years as a cook and had no idea how to cook. One day, he decided to come in the galley and make fried rice. His first mistake was not wearing a hat. His second mistake, after putting the rice and vegetables on the griddle, was dowsing it with almost a half gallon of soy sauce.

There was so much liquid that the rice became overcooked and tasted like mush. It was as salty as the sea we were sailing on and there was no way that I was going to serve this to the crew. My first mistake was making him leave to go get a hat instead of getting one for him. I figured he should know better and he probably figured I should know better. My second mistake was telling him his rice was unfit for human consumption and we would serve white rice instead.

I proceeded to dump the rice into the trash can in front of him trying to make it look as if it was breaking my heart. All the soy sauce had burnt onto the griddle so I dumped a bucket of ice on it to loosen it up and the crackle of the ice made for quite the dramatic scene as the rest of the crew looked on.

I should have handled it better and, in retrospect, I could have been more diplomatic in my approach. It was stupid of me to make him look bad but at the time I thought he only made himself look bad.

When the Captain wanted me to work for him, Master Chief didn't have a say in the matter and I could tell that also bugged him.

Master Chief spent his early Navy years cleaning staterooms for officers before becoming an administrative cook doing record keeping and working in barracks. After that, he got a job at the Navy Annex where he stayed for half of his career and getting promoted along the way without ever knowing how to cook. I thought that was unacceptable and still do.

"Master Chief," I said "The Navy wants to talk to me about working in Washington, so I have to go up to DC for a few days."

I downplayed the whole situation. I didn't want him making any phone calls if you know what I mean. He was just the type to do so.

We were out at sea that next day and were pulling into Boston just in time for me to go to DC for my interview screening. My wife Christina met me in Boston so we could go to DC together. We drove down through the night and stayed at the Sheraton immediately next to the Navy Annex, which sat on a hill overlooking part of Arlington National Cemetery and the Pentagon.

It was the first time either of us had seen Washington and we were excited about the possibility of living there. Christina helped me prepare for my interview while we ordered room service for breakfast and I ironed my uniform for my meeting in a few hours. I wasn't nervous until I walked into the Annex building and made my way to the office to begin the interview process, along with seven other cooks that were interviewing for the same job.

After a few minutes of sitting, the tiredness of driving through the night started taking effect and I became more relaxed. We ended up piling into a van and were brought to the Old Executive Office Building (OEOB) which houses the administrative offices to support the White House.

The building was impressive. A gothic, French style building built of solid concrete to prevent from being burned down and suffer the same fate as the original White House during the war of 1812. We were ushered in through Secret Service one at a time and lead up to the third floor where there was a military office. This office was the nucleus of all military personnel that support the President.

The Air Force handles the flying of the President on board their aircraft. The Marines fly him on their helicopters. The Army handles communications between the President and the Joint Chiefs of Staff and the Navy handles the food service.

My first interview was with a Navy Commander and an Army Major. Both were military aides to Vice President Dan Quayle, who was Vice President under George H.W. Bush. The questions at first were more focused on my military training and background. Then they moved on to what life was like growing up and how I feel about working for the Captain on board ship.

After the interview was over, we all waited for each of us to take a turn with the aides, until all of us had finished the first part of the screening. We were sizing each other up. Making small talk and talking about ports of call while quietly checking over each others ribbons on our dress blue uniforms to see who is really the best qualified on the outside.

We were given instructions for the next day's proceedings and told we would be taken to the Vice President's house, which is based in the Naval Observatory in Washington DC in an area known as Embassy Row. Everyone was excited that we all passed the first interview and cordially said goodbye to each other as we got dropped off back at the Annex.

The next day, we piled back in the van and headed to the house. We were met by the Master Chief in charge and ushered in to the kitchen where they were preparing a lunch for Marilyn Quayle and around 20 guests. I saw a familiar face while walking into the kitchen. It was Petty Officer Kermit Apple, a guy I worked with in Italy who started working at the VP's house around four months ago. Kermit was a great guy and it was great to see him.

After a brief introduction to the rest of the crew, I looked over the menu for the luncheon and of course, remembering first impressions, asked if there was anything I could do to help. I was politely told that they had it under control.

Master Chief went on to talk to all of us about their day to day work load and how important it was to take care of the Quayle's kids and maintain the kitchen pantries on each floor for the kids. He seemed to go on and on about the kids and I was starting to think I'd be a nanny rather than a cook.

There was no real focus on our cooking skills and I was sizing up where I would be on the rank of the other cooks in the kitchen. Yep, I would be the junior guy and thoughts of washing dishes in Italy started swirling in my head. I wouldn't mind cooking for the kids, since as long as I was cooking I would be happy. Doing laundry and other duties are par for the course but it wasn't looking like I'd be cooking at all. Kermit was a great cook, but it didn't sound like he was doing much cooking.

We were then prepped by the Master Chief for our next phase of the interview process. An interview with Marilyn Quayle's personal aide, a civilian lady that pretty much ran the house.

She was a very well manicured and attractive African-American lady that had a warm personality and polite demeanor about her. She put me at ease right away and we talked at first as though we were old acquaintances catching up after not seeing each other for years. The interview, I thought, was going great. She was asking all the right questions but still not touching on my cooking abilities. In my head, all I could do was think of what Master Chief was saying about the kids and how important it was to take care of them and I was curious to see if this conversation was going to go in that very same direction. It didn't take long.

She started asking if I had kids. How I interact with kids and so on. By now, I kind of knew what was up and didn't like what I was hearing. I was, to be honest, disappointed and felt like this was a complete waste of time but I had to play along. At least until I could tell my wife that this was a crap gig and get her on board with what I was thinking, which was to turn down this job. It was voluntary and the Navy could not make me do it.

Then I had a moment of genius. I don't know why I didn't thought of it ten minutes before. I lied in order to not get the job. I was so proud of myself.

"Do you know how to iron?" The aide said and thoughts of ironing kid's clothes went through my head. Of course I do. I did all the ironing at home. My Mum, who was in the dressmaking and kilt making business, taught me how and I always iron my own clothes. Even on the ship. I can sew, I can crochet, I can needlepoint and pretty much do anything domesticated. Put me up against any Chinese laundry and I will give them a run for the money. Do I iron?

"No," I replied. A bold face and blatant lie that should I have been hooked up to one of those machines with the cords around my chest and fingers, the needle would have deviated so sharp off course it would have sounded like RUN DMC were scratching records.

"Well then, thank you for your time and it was nice to meet you," was her response and the interview was over. Now, I don't know if that was the last question she had planned for the interview or if it went on and on with more menial tasks but it was my last question and I was glad it was.

When I met up with Christina that afternoon, she was anxious to hear how it went. I filled her in on everything and told her it did not go well. I blew it. I then went on to explain why and she couldn't believe I said I couldn't iron. To this day I still iron all of her clothes as well as my own.

We both agreed that tomorrow I would let them know that I am no longer interested in the opportunity and thank them for the chance to be picked to serve the Vice President and his family. We ended up going to a little diner down the road for dinner and planned what would we do next. We talked about other places we both wanted to see and put together our own dream sheet of sorts to feel better about the day. I couldn't help but feel disappointed.

On the next day we all assembled again at the Annex and were driven to the Old Executive Office Building again. We waited around for what seemed like an eternity then were handed slips of paper with a time on it. We were free to do what we wanted and had to be back at the time prescribed on the paper so I decided to walk around the White House since it was next door and I had never seen it before this trip.

While walking, I thought about how to sound professional in turning down the rest of the process and pretty much telling the aides

I'm not interested. I had to do it in a way that the detailer would still help me find another job rather than think I wasn't worth it and tell me to stay in Norfolk.

After a nice slow stroll around the White House, I ended up back at the OEOB. I was admiring the architecture and thought this building is by far more impressive than what I saw of the White House. It was like a building out of a movie and immersed in history. I guess what I was also trying to do was find a distraction from quitting the interview process. I was a wreck inside and afraid of any repercussion from rejecting the job.

Well, time was up and I had to face the music. I stepped into the office of the military aides and after shaking their hands took a seat on the couch facing both the Commander and Major.

The major began with saying, "Petty Officer Macfarlane, we have decided to move forward with another candidate and we are both very thankful on behalf of the Vice President and his staff that you were kind enough to interview for this position."

Music to my blooming ears, I thought to myself. They each went on to say how well qualified I was and this should not reflect anything wrong on my part and I should be proud of my service in the Navy. They really knew how to let a guy down gently and I was beginning to feel as if I should still fight to stay in the race. They were that good.

After a few minutes talking, I think they just wanted to make sure I was OK and not going to snap, they asked me what my plans were for the future. I told them that my wife was here in town with me and that we would spend the next day in DC sightseeing before I went back to the ship and try to get orders for my shore duty rotation.

They both looked at each other and then the commander spoke. "Would you be interested in another job here? Not at the Vice President's house," he asked with his hands out toward me as if to say please.

"Yes sir," I responded "What do you have in mind?"

"We also have a job that you would be perfect for. It is in the White House Staff Mess and you would be working with the best chef's in the Navy. Are you interested?"

"Yes sir, very much so. Do they do their own cooking there or are there civilians that do that?" I asked just to make sure.

"They do all their own cooking as well as travel with the President wherever in the world he goes," said the major.

"Yes sir, I am very interested. What do I need to do?"

"Hang tight and we'll see if we can get you in this afternoon. We both think you would be better suited for this position versus the other," the major said.

I was feeling much better and excited about the possibility to cook in the White House. This is every chef's dream. This is the ultimate job and would be a great job if I can get it. While I waited, I reflected on how I was not selected for the Vice President's job. This was the first time in my life that I did not get a job that I was qualified for but then I remembered I wasn't qualified. "I cannot iron," I thought with a smile coming to my face.

It wasn't long before the aides returned. They both thanked me once again and escorted me into another office up on the fourth floor in the south east corner of the building. It was the White House Staff Mess office and was run by the Navy. I was met by a Yeoman at the front desk and then by a Senior Chief that did the hiring and recruiting for cooks, but was surprised that he was a Yeoman also and not a cook.

He went over my service record that was given to him by the military aides to the Vice President. They already put in a good word for me and we set up a time for me to come back and interview for the White House job. We made it for the following month. I then departed and gave my wife the good news. The next night we headed back to Norfolk with a feeling of anxiousness the whole way there.

Captain Brewer was anxious to hear how it went and fill him in on all the details. I proceeded to tell him that I was now being asked to interview for the White House and that I didn't get the job at the Vice President's house. He was happy for me and wrote me a glowing letter of recommendation for the job. This carried a lot of weight when I went back to DC and interviewed. He also coached me on how to have a successful interview prior to me going to DC and I was extremely grateful he did. I must admit that his help and support got me the job.

My wife and I were moving to Washington and I was in for one of the most rewarding jobs of my life.

Everybody was proud of me for getting the job. Especially my wife. She later received a letter from the office of the Vice President expressing how she should be proud of my accomplishments and how grateful they were that I interviewed to work for Vice President Quayle. This token of sincere gratitude was a really nice touch and helped us both value the opportunity to serve the office of the President and Vice President.

Captain Brewer left the ship a couple of weeks before I did. He was going to Washington DC for a short tour in the Pentagon while waiting for his promotion to Rear Admiral. A promotion he duly deserved.

I learned a lot from being around him so much, especially how to be an effective leader. Every good chef needs to be a leader in order to be able to manage a kitchen and its staff and Captain Brewer helped me take my leadership skills to the next level.

Before he left he put me in to receive a Navy Achievement Medal for the work I did aboard the ship. I never looked at what I had done as anything special. I looked at it as though I was only doing what I was meant to do. When I read his recommendation, I could not help but feel proud to have served with him and thinking of my career and future with a new family.

My Master Chief held on to the paperwork for my award until after the Captain transferred off the ship. Then, it was pay back time. He stood in front a group of my fellow cooks aboard ship, held up the recommendation form from the Captain and ripped it into pieces while professing his dislike for me publicly.

It wasn't long before word got back to me of what just happened. The other cooks used to talk about how stupid Master Chief was behind his back but I never thought to join in those conversations. Heck, I was probably one they talked about also when I wasn't in the room. Anyway, none of them could believe what had happened and probably realized that he would do the same to them if given the chance.

This guy only cared about himself and no one else, and in this act of immaturity and disgust only confirmed I had made the right choice of staying away from him. He was everything I detested in a boss. Selfish, self serving, ignorant and, most of all, uncaring.

By doing what he did, he cost me my next promotion. He knew that by not getting any recognition from my previous command, once leaving, that I was just an average sailor and nothing special. Even if I was going to the White House, a move that made him dislike me more, he knew what he was doing.

I never brought it up or tried to get the medal after I was told what happened. I saw Captain Brewer many times after this happened and never once told him that I never got my award and what the Master Chief had done. I let it go. Even though I was angry at first, I just let it go. I had no control over the situation and it went through all the proper channels before ending up on Master Chief's desk, I thought. Who am I to tell him what to do? Nobody.

After my tour on the ship was up, my security clearance was still not complete. The detailer cut me orders to work in the Pentagon in the meantime at the office of the Chief of Naval Operations. The highest ranking Admiral in the Navy. I wasn't there long before my clearance went through but at the Pentagon I worked with some of the finest sailors that I ever met. It was a great experience and yes, they let me cook.

I had a great time working with Mr. Miranda (retired Master Chief) and the rest of the crew there. Senior Chief Pederson, my immediate boss, turned out to be one of my biggest fans. He was sad to see me leave but I made time to visit him regularly. He loved to cook and we shared a lot of recipes with each other. He was the one that gave me a recipe for a canapé that was so simple and so delicious that I had to make it whenever the opportunity arrived.

Take two cups of diced fresh Spanish onion. Mix in one cup of regular mayonnaise and one cup of shredded parmesan cheese. Once fully incorporated, set aside. Preheat oven to three fifty. Cut the crusts off of some sliced white bread and then cut into triangles. Arrange on a sheet tray and spoon the onion mixture onto each triangle of bread. Garnish with some paprika and parsley and bake until bubbly and the bread is toasted. Eat and enjoy.

My wife and kids still love these "Onion Puffs" whenever I make them.

# THE WHITE HOUSE

On my first day at the White House I met my new division officer, a Supply Lieutenant. He seemed rather stand offish at first and I thought that maybe he was just feeling awkward since he was new also and had never met me before. He wasn't the one who I interviewed with and he was meeting me for the first time. He was a submariner just like most of the other cooks on staff. Come to find out he thought really highly of himself and really lowly of everybody else. That was just the way he was.

Everybody used to complain about him behind his back but was overly nice to his face. I never played that game and stayed as far away from him as possible. I wasn't there trying to get a promotion or a commission, I was there to cook and that is all I wanted to do.

The Lieutenant put me in logistics. There were four departments that supported the President. Logistics, the galley, the Oval Office steward and the valets who took care of the President's wardrobe.

Logistics was run by Master Chief Nelvis and Senior Chief Francisco. Both were great guys and a pleasure to work with. My job was to pick up the food orders that we would place at various suppliers around the Washington DC area that had been approved by the Secret Service. We drove vans around town picking up produce, liquor, meats, breads and more.

Deliveries were not allowed so we had to get our own and also do so incognito. We no longer wore military uniforms and wore civilian shirts with ties and slacks. There were about five others that worked in logistics and we were all pretty new. Senior Chief Francisco and I were the only surface sailors. The others were all Bubble Heads (submariners).

Our day started at 5:30 in the morning and ended around 4pm. Depending, of course, on the work load and how many runs we would have to do. We would then pull the products that the kitchen would order and put the products in carts. Our office was in the basement of the Old Executive Office Building and we would cart the products over to the basement of the West Wing, where the kitchen and dining rooms were.

We would also pack trunks of food and drinks that would be used to support the President when he was traveling outside of the White House. The Navy is solely responsible for supporting all facets of the Office of the President in performing his or her duties as President.

It all started when, according to the White House Military Office, that Navy stewards (cooks) first served the Office of the President aboard the Presidential Yacht Despatch during the presidency of Rutherford B. Hayes. Franklin D. Roosevelt then established the Presidential Retreat known as Shangri-La (which is now Camp David) and utilized Navy cooks to staff the mess. In 1951, Rear Admiral Dennison was an aide to President Truman when he suggested an Officers' Mess be established at the White House. It was then that the White House Mess was established and the Navy has 'Manned the Rails' ever since.

Presidential Food Service has a long and distinguished history with the very top one percent of Navy cooks carrying on the tradition.

It was a pleasure for me to be chosen for such a prestigious position as well as an honor to be accepted.

Logistics wasn't exactly what I thought I would be doing at the White House but I wasn't complaining. I was happy to have the job and happy to move my wife and son up from Norfolk to a small apartment in Virginia until we found something permanent, which we later did. A beautiful, little beach house right on the Chesapeake Bay in Maryland. It was extremely relaxing and even though it was farther from work, it was still quicker to get home in the evenings than driving south into Virginia.

By the time I was becoming comfortable with logistics, my wife became pregnant with our second son, Andrew Sean. I was starting to travel with the President and starting to really enjoy the type of work I was doing. Even though important, I never looked at it as so. I looked at it as, "Maybe tomorrow they will ask me to cook."

Cooking is all I wanted to do. The kitchen was tiny and only manned by three cooks on the hot line, plus one on salad and one on sandwiches. It was designed by submarine engineers and extremely claustrophobic if you weren't used to tight spaces. When President Bush was in office we fed, on average, 80 people in both dining rooms and carry out service. The Oval Office stewards would pick up the tray for the President and feed him topside in a dining room adjacent to the Oval Office.

When President Clinton became President we went from 80 to around 240 almost instantly. President Clinton opened our services to almost everybody on his staff rather than just the upper cabinet members as it was under President Bush. This was a sure sign of the difference between administrations and kept us busy all day.

I would hang out in the kitchen after taking the food there each day to check out what they were cooking. Three main entrees a day, about six salad choices, a daily special, three soups and about a dozen sandwich options. It wasn't long before I was sizing myself up against who was cooking and thinking of what I would do differently.

Lunch was the main meal and we did two sittings. One at 11:30 and another at 12:45. That gave no room for error and the meals had to crank out. Senior Chief Smith, the kitchen boss, was the expediter and his job was to make sure every plate was perfect on time. He was a great guy to work with and a great sailor to know. He was always looking for ways to improve the menu each day and loved what he did.

Every chance I got to take a break from logistics, I would wander the halls of the Old Executive Office Building to admire the architecture. It was designed by Alfred B. Mullett and is a very French looking design, built around 1880.

One day, while wandering around, I found the jewel which captured my attention immediately and soon became my favorite room in the building. The Presidential Law Library. The room was lined with books. Lots of books. It had a wrought iron rail around each floor with narrow black iron spiral staircases. In my opinion, it was the most beautiful room in the building and soon became my own private oasis where I could think and read every chance I got.

I never shared with anybody what I had found. I wanted to keep it all to myself and it was hardly ever used. I would grab some coffee and take the stairs to the library. I would thumb through the law reference books and was reminded of my childhood. Imagine how surprised I was by this. I was more than 3,000 miles from home at the epicenter of power in the free world, surrounded by books as important as the office who uses them and I am reminded of how hard it was growing up.

"How did I end up here?" I would wonder to myself. "Would my Dad be proud of me? Is my Mum proud of me? Had I done the right things in life? Did I choose the right profession?" All these thoughts would go through my head as if rushing in and completely wiping out the day-to-day stress of the job. For the first time in my life, I reflected on what I had done instead of focusing on what I wanted to do. It was almost life changing in a sense.

I love the subject of law. From Leviticus to the commercial codes of law today, I have always been fascinated by its language, history and effects on mankind. From God's Law to common law, our lives cannot escape it. We are bound by it and tried by it should we break it. When Moses received the Ten Commandments in stone, written by the finger of God himself, he gave us law. Not suggestions. Not a caution and certainly not, "Please do this." He handed down the law. It amazed me how in school, the most important indoctrination into a civilized society, we never learned about law. We never learned about Acts, Statutes or Ordinances or the difference thereof. No mention was made of the jurisdiction of common law versus Admiralty law. Our very lives could be at stake and we didn't know the law. Yet ignorance is no defense. How silly is that.

My time in logistics was a great experience. We had a good crew and, most of all, good leadership. On Friday afternoons we had time to take our ties off and drink some beer while listening to Master Chief Nelvis belt out a few Neil Diamond songs on the karaoke machine he kept in one of the cabinets. We had food and snacks all over the room and people from around the building knew every Friday logistics was the place to be. It was always good fun but I would catch the first van out of there to get home to my pregnant wife and baby, to spend some much needed time together. Coming from sea duty this was no cake walk but sure nice to be home.

We would travel with the President everywhere he went outside the gates of the White House, even if it was down the street to the Capitol Building. We would go ahead of him, depending on the trip, sometimes a day or two, and fly on the Air Force cargo planes loaded with his limo and Secret Service detail. We would get to know those guys pretty well and took good care of each other with the benefits of the job like free food in hotels to review the menu or slipping them some boxes of M&Ms with the President's signature on them to hand out as a thank you to the local Secret Service helping out.

We would carry water for the President in oversized brief cases that resembled the ones pilots wheel around with their luggage and are packed full of airport protocol manuals. Every where we went, people would think we were carrying the launch codes for a nuclear strike, which is referred to as "The Football." And you couldn't help but notice the points and the stares. If they only knew.

Very rarely did we ever get the chance to fly Air Force One. But one day, I got lucky while on a trip to Kansas City. There happened to be an opening for me to ride in luxury back home instead of on the cargo plane.

We made an unscheduled stop on our way to Kansas City Airport. The President decided he wanted some barbecue. So the motorcade of about eleven cars, not including the police escorts, veered off course and headed to one of Kansas City's most famous barbecue restaurants, Gates Bar B.Q. If you've never eaten at Gates then you are missing some great food. I was so glad we stopped.

Once we arrived, I jumped out of the van and headed right to the kitchen. My job on the road was to make sure there are no dodgy practices going on in any of the kitchens and, most of all, that nobody tries to mess with the food that the President is about to eat. Since this was an unscheduled stop, I could not arrive ahead of the President so he was already inside rubbing palms with everybody in between him and what he really came for. The barbecue!

I quickly jumped in the back where the kitchen was and snaked my way around the prep tables looking for anything out of the ordinary. Next stop was looking through the coolers then onto the trash cans. I moved them all out of the way and toward the back wall away from the food. After looking over the smokers next I couldn't help but think about eating myself. There isn't a better smell than pork ribs and beef brisket getting smoked at 177 degrees Fahrenheit. It is heavenly, with an overwhelming power to call out to all of ones senses to partake in this rotisserie of sheer pleasure.

Everything looked good and before you know it Mr. Clinton was elbow deep in a full plate of barbecue. It was really quite evident that he was enjoying the food just as much as the restaurant workers were enjoying seeing him. About 40 minutes later we were back on the road and headed to the ride of all rides.

Once on board Air Force One it was fantastic. I sat near the tail section in front of the crew seats and savored every minute of a two hour flight that I didn't want to end. It was truly a fantastic ride and I would have never guessed in my wildest dreams how luxurious it was.

Every seat on board was oversized and overstuffed. I was handed a list of movies and told to call the communications room with my choice of movie. It would pop up on the screen I pulled out of the arm rest. There was a nice size conference room on board as well as a medical room that had just about every piece of medical equipment imaginable.

The President had his own cabin in the nose of the converted Boeing 747 with a Secret Service agent posted immediately outside his door. There were two kitchens on board and nothing like my old kitchen on the P-3. These kitchens were huge but the cooks didn't use the spaces to cook, just reheat from what I saw. I assumed they prepped everything on the ground, and then brought the food on board in refrigerated trolleys.

As soon as the President was on board we didn't wait around for anything or anybody else. We started rolling with one engine on and the rest to follow while taxiing to the runway. In what seemed like seconds, we were rotating and in the air quicker than I had ever been before. It was a fantastic experience. A few weeks later I received a certificate from the Air Force in recognition of my flight aboard Air Force One as a guest of Bill Clinton. This, I thought, was a nice touch.

At this point, I loved every aspect of my job but continued to read every cooking magazine I could find as well as carry my third edition of The Professional Chef book from the Culinary Institute of

America everywhere I went. I did this so I could always think about cooking and not forget anything I learned. I was always afraid of losing what I knew, especially since I hadn't cooked in so long.

Visiting resorts and hotels, where I could never afford to visit, helped me dramatically expand my culinary knowledge as well as allow me to venture into new and exotic foods that were a far cry from cooking a Cornish game hen on the ship. I would read menus every where I went and emerge myself in understanding the French terms of cookery beyond the basics I learned in school.

Pierre Chambrin was the head chef for the First Family within the residence of the White House. He was a classically trained French Chef and a master at his art. Whichever chef holds this position gets all the press and fame from working in the White House and is always heralded as America's Chef.

Chef Pierre had a staff of two Sous Chefs, John and Sean. I am still in touch with Chef Pierre and John to this day. Chef Pierre also had a pastry chef under him who was called Rolland Messier. Chef Roland was a master at sugar work and everything he made looked like porcelain sculptures because of his extreme attention to detail. At first glance, I found it hard to believe these works of art were made from sugar. I had seen sugar work before but his was above anything I could imagine. I wanted desperately to watch how he did this and possibly try my own hand at learning from a master but his kitchen was too small to accommodate me in addition to the two ladies that worked with him. He worked out of a closet and that is not an understatement. The room was on the third floor of the residence and reminded me of the small kitchens in Europe. A micro kitchen decorated in cold white tile walls with equipment squeezed in only to leave enough room to walk around baker's racks of every kind of pan necessary for a world class pastry chef like Roland. Chef Roland was a delight to get to know.

I would read the resident chef's menus from time to time and volunteer to be their commis chef should they need someone to peel carrots or prep food for large functions. I would do any and all the menial tasks they would ask from me. It didn't matter. I wasn't too proud to wash pots and pans to help out, I never have been nor ever will be.

I never liked when people thought they were too good to clean or even too good to cook. It was a clear sign to me of a lack of caring in my opinion. I believe in setting the example in a kitchen, not just dictating authority and feeling you're too good or too important to clean. In my opinion, clean dishes are important. A paperweight? Not so much.

They would always take me up on my offer and teach me the French terms for whatever I was working on and I would give them my all in return. This was the kitchen of all kitchens with chefs that were envied by all chefs. And here I was, a wee ginger kid from East Kilbride, standing elbow to elbow with the best in the world. Turning potatoes by the bucketful and telling jokes to keep from counting potatoes.

Who I was cooking for didn't matter to me. Who I was cooking with, did.

On one occasion, the White House was hosting the largest garden party ever in the history of the presidency. We were setting up to feed 5,000 guests on the South Lawn and had to pull it off with six manned chef stations and four Army field kitchens. What an experience!

Before we manned our stations, the White House photographer wanted to get a picture of us to record this historical moment. We stood there proud of what we were doing but you could tell our minds were someplace else. We were all thinking of what still needed done and we wouldn't be happy until the night was over and each of the 5,000 guests were fed to our complete satisfaction. We still had a lot to do.

The six stations were set up three a side, inside a large tent. There were two field kitchens at each side. The stations were set up in the order in which to support the chef's stations. It was all hands on deck. The chefs from the Blair House even came over to help, as well as chefs from all the embassies in town, since they all had security clearances which were hard to get and proved they could be trusted.

We had to make up 12 speed racks holding 22 trays each of canapés. After that we made 20 lexans of salad and then moved onto roasting beef tenderloins to be carved at each of the six stations and held in hot boxes next to the field kitchens, where we were making up the sides and frying finger foods for the wait staff to pass with the canapés. It was a lot of work and about four days of preparation.

Chef Pierre was going around from station to station checking up on everyone with his walkie-talkie in hand and helping to do whatever needed done. All in all, there was a lot going on for everyone involved and it was great to be a part of. After the function, we all took about 15 minutes to sit around an aluminum fishing boat filled with ice and beer and joined the party. It was one of those nights where you look around in amazement and wonder if this is really happening. "Am I really here doing this?" I couldn't believe it but, "Yes." I was there and I was really doing what I wanted to do most in life, and having a beer on the South Lawn of the White House, with my feet propped up on a boat full of beer.

# LIVING THE DREAM

Before I knew it, I got the call to leave logistics and do what I was meant to do in life. Cook! I was so happy. Trading in the shirt and tie for some chef whites was exactly what I wanted and you would have thought I had just won the lottery. The only other person who knew how I felt was Archie Gemmill, when he scored against Holland at the 1978 World Cup in Argentina. I was ecstatic.

I was now one of three on the hotline. Work started at five in the morning to feed the crew by nine and the guests by 11:30. There were no easy days. This was hard work but I was ready for it. I did everything I could to prove this is where I belonged rather than driving all day to pick up fish.

The orders would pile in and we would crank them out as fast as possible. It wasn't long before you could feel yourself getting in the weeds as Senior Chief Smith peered through the shelves with the hot lamps at all the tickets you had hanging without saying a word. He didn't need to. We all knew what he was thinking and he knew we knew as well. Saying anything wasn't going to help unless you were really in the crap and couldn't dig your way out with a snow shovel. His stare was enough of a message.

We would make all the soups on our duty Saturday which came every third Saturday of the month. On my first duty day, I was given my prep list from Senior Chief Smith, who worked every Saturday, and I happily went through it on my own.

- Debone two cases of chicken.
- Roast bones, make stock.

- Make consommé of chicken.

- Make beef stock.

- Make tomato bullion.

- Roast and peel peppers.

- Make mirepoix.

- Make tomato concasse.

- Precook and portion pasta.

- Peel and devein shrimp and portion into bags with marinade.

- Make croutons.

- Drain and clean fryer, fill with fresh oil.

The list was easy and I had six hours to get it done. Plenty of time I thought and went straight to work. Later on one of the guys working the sandwich line that day told me "Senior Chief doesn't want me to help you if you ask, just so you know." "I didn't need any help anyway," I thought to myself. I didn't know if he was kidding or serious since I didn't know the guy at all and I wasn't going to need help anyway. I never found out if he was serious or not because I was done way earlier than even I first thought possible and double checked everything before asking the Senior Chief what else I could do.

I enjoyed getting back to cooking and before long I started to compete in culinary competitions through the local chapter of the American Culinary Federation. This allowed me to develop my presentation skills and start networking with the local chefs.

I did my best to focus on giving back to the industry by working with the student chefs from local high schools around DC and Maryland. It was gratifying to see how much they appreciated actual working chefs spending time with them and allowed me to help develop kids' skills in cookery. It allowed me to be a part of continuing the long tradition of passing our knowledge on to the next generation.

It wasn't long before my Mum came to visit us in Maryland and I could give her a tour of the White House. I did my very best to ensure she would enjoy the experience as much as possible and somehow remind her of our breakfasts together at the diner in New Jersey. Her 54th birthday was coming up and I had a surprise for her.

I arranged to get a couple of seats at the President's Box in the Kennedy Center of Performing Arts. Before the show, I arranged for my Mum to have dinner in the White House dining room with my wife Christina before going to the play. I couldn't go since I was working that night anyway.

I created their own special menus and made a feast for them both of everything I could think of to impress my Mum. I wanted to show her how far I had come in life and how proud she could be of me for sticking to cooking and not looking for an easy way through life. From Parkhill to Pennsylvania Avenue, we had all come a long way. She had a right to be proud of herself, since she made it through all those tough times we had together and raised all of her kids by herself. Now, she was having dinner in the most exclusive private dining rooms in the world and I had the pleasure to cater to the two most important women in my life.

The menu consisted of:

- Grilled Prawn Salad in an orange vinaigrette over micro green salad. The prawns were marinated in Mrs. Clinton's favorite marinade, orange juice, garlic and a little soy sauce and olive oil.

- Maryland Crab Cakes with cucumber relish and confetti sweet peppers with a Creole remoulade sauce.
- Key Lime Sorbet and Sweet Berry Compote.
- Slow Roasted Flank Steak with Pomme Nouvelle and Baby Vegetables.
- Assorted Petit Fours and Cafe Americana.

I felt more proud serving my Mum and my wife that evening than I did for anybody else ever in my life. Senior Chief Smith stayed behind to help me since he knew how important this was for all of us. He was a great help since I was more nervous than I had ever been before in my life. This night had to be perfect in order to pull this off. I wanted her to forget about everything we had been through together. I wanted her to feel like the most important person in the world that night. Happy birthday Mum!

By now, I was cooking full days in the West Wing, traveling on short notice whenever needed and studying for my next promotion. And then I got asked if I wanted to work part time at the Blair House, which is located across the street from the White House and serves as the President's Guest House.

The first thing I thought of was that my wife was going to kill me if I took on another job and she was stuck home with an infant and another one on the way. But reality was, we needed the money.

Even though I worked at the White House, I still got paid my Navy salary. By leaving the ship, I lost almost $400 a month of extra sea pay and, with another child on the way, I could barely afford to pass this chance up. I already worked some jobs for the resident chefs and made $18 an hour to do so. Problem was, there wasn't enough work to have a steady income. The Blair House opportunity was steady work and we needed the money.

I decided to take the time to go across Pennsylvania Avenue one afternoon and meet Chef Russell Kronkite, Executive Chef of the Blair House, and see what exactly he was looking for as well as find out if it was what I needed.

Chef Russell was a large man with the frame of a builder. Turned out, before becoming a chef, he was a construction worker in Colorado. He stood about six two and had a grip like a vice. When I shook his hand it was like grabbing a bunch of bananas. Thick hands and fingers lead me to think, "I wouldn't want to scrap with this guy." He had long brown hair and a trimmed beard to match. The one thing that stands out to me the most about Chef was that he wore a white neckerchief tied around his neck in the classical French way you don't see anymore. It was something you're forced to do in school and that was it, unless of course you drew the short straw at work and had to attend to a sauté or carving station during a banquet. A job that no self respecting chef ever wants.

Chef Russell asked me if I wanted any coffee. I politely accepted. My biggest weakness is that I cannot pass on the coffee. I hardly drink alcohol and for that I get a lot of stick, especially being in the Navy and for being Scottish where both categories have a reputation for being heavy drinkers. My vice is coffee. I love it, a lot.

I wish I was better prepared for this meeting since I looked chef over his nice clean chef whites and I looked like a slob having

179

just finished the lunch rush and shuffled directly over to the Blair House without changing out of my lightly soiled chef coat. I apologized for my appearance, I wanted to set a good first impression of course, and tried not to let it bother me but it did.

After getting our coffee we proceeded to go to his office and have a seat to discuss him bringing me on board whenever he needed me. I took my first sip of coffee after looking at the collection of cookbooks he had lined up on the book shelves next to his desk. You can tell a lot about a chef by which books he keeps. His style will become evident by the titles and authors displayed and a good indication of the style of cooking he prefers. Escoffier's Le Guide Culinaire was the first book I noticed. It was a book published in 1903 by the father of modern French cuisine, Auguste Escoffier. This is the bible for chefs and although sometimes only used as a prop in some offices, I could tell that Chef Russell referred to it regularly by its position on the shelf closest to his desk and the worn binding holding a wealth of knowledge together that was indented at the top where his large finger would pull it towards him.

I took my first sip of coffee and fell in love. "What kind of coffee is this chef?" I asked as I headed in for a second sip. "It is delicious."

The coffee was a strong as Russell's grip. I had a flash of Italy before my eyes and the aroma was similar to the Baristos that I became so accustomed to frequent, like an alcoholic bellying up to the bar in anticipation of a fix.

"It's my own special blend that I have roasted for me," Chef replied as he dove into his cup.

It put my mind at ease and helped me loosen up for what I thought was just an introductory meeting but turned into an interview. Chef asked me about what I liked to cook. What was my favorite cuisine and, more importantly, if I was dependable.

I told him everything I had ever done. Being a baker's apprentice, cooking at home, reading cookbooks as much as possible and what I did on board ship for the Captain. I told him about my love affair with Italy and before long we were both sharing our stories as if parked on Memory Lane and having a picnic with a flask of the most delicious coffee I have had in years.

We ended up having a lot in common. He too, learned the hard way. He loved to cook and loved to talk about foods from all over the world. Chef Russell wasn't just the first real chef I would work for; he was the first culinary perfectionist I had ever worked under.

I was hired by Chef Russell to work evenings whenever the President had guests stay at the Blair House. The kitchen staff was only Chef and his pastry chef Kim. Everybody else was hired on an 'as needed' basis and we were paid $28 dollars an hour. A sum that more than made up for my loss of sea pay.

Ian was the lead kitchen temp and whom I would be working for in the hot kitchen. He was a giant of a man and from Manchester, England. He used to work at the British Embassy before taking this job under Chef Russell and he was a maniac in the kitchen. And I mean maniac in a good way.

Ian was one of the most hard working chefs I'd come to know. He was a true professional with a tenacious spirit to ensure the guests are happy and the food is perfect. My first day working for Ian left me with sore legs, sore hands and a sore back. I felt like I was in a fight and when I got home at midnight that night I didn't fall asleep, I passed out. He worked me harder than anyone had ever done before. Harder than even Willie.

Ian gave me a prep list to make all his mise en place for the dinner service as well as make a staff meal from the leftover foods from the previous day. Nobody ever pays for a staff meal so you have to make it with whatever scraps you have left over and it better be bloody good. If the staff dislikes your cooking, you're sunk. You will never recover and never have the ability to redeem yourself. They will always remember the bad meal and never let you forget it. The staff meal can make or break a cook and they are the toughest critics alive.

At the Blair House we made everything from scratch. Take for example, if we had petit pois on the menu we would start with shucking the peas out of their pods. Peel and blanch the pearl onions. Debone chickens and roast the bones for the stock. It was an experience I will never forget.

We would make all of our own stocks and my particular favorite was the veal stock we would make for the demi-glace. I love the smell of veal stock. We would roast the shank bones then braise them in a bath of water, billowing with carrots, onions, celery, bay leaf and peppercorn. The aroma was amazing. The stock would cook for hours it seemed until we got the flavor and color just right. A nice light chestnut brown would be perfect and strained through a china cap first then a chinoise (a fine mesh strainer) to catch smaller particles and the peppercorns before chilling the stock in the refrigerator. I would make a meal of the discarded vegetables and soaked up the juices with some bread from the pastry kitchen. The next day the liquid would turn into wobbly-looking jello because of the gelatinous marrow cooked from the shanks. Heavenly stuff!

The pastry kitchen was also a great place to work. We made our own chocolate truffles and just about every type of classical French torte imaginable was on the menu. We baked our own bread, made our own fruit fillings and custards as well as make our own fondant and marzipan decorations. This was, in my eyes, the type of food that made the pain of working two jobs worthwhile.

Even though the Blair House is not as familiar as the White House to most people, it is very important to the President. His guests stay there when visiting and we mostly catered to Presidents and Prime Ministers from around the globe and a few Kings for good measure.

Not just any chef could work at the Blair House. You had to have a higher clearance than we did at the White House due to the importance of catering to foreign leaders. Every chef was hand picked, not only for their ability to cook under this immense pressure but for their ability to achieve the highest standards fit to serve Presidents, Prime Ministers and Royalty.

Chef Russell would fret over every detail of the meals we produced and would follow the servers to the pantry and ensure the foods were perfectly arranged on the silver French platters as if to align perfectly with the planets of the universe to prevent the Earth from wobbling off of its orbit. That's how serious he took it. I loved this about him.

We often got thank you presents from the visiting guests and one time I received a beautiful Egyptian silk tie and a crisp one hundred dollar bill peeled off of a layered stack of crisp notes that I was amazed to see from President Mubarak of Egypt. I had never seen so much money in one place in my life. I took my wife to a much needed and much deserved lunch date with the cash and proudly showed her my tie. She put it in the pile of other ties I had hanging in the closet and politely asked if President Mubarak was coming back again soon. I couldn't help but laugh.

About a week later she decided to wash all of my ties. Big mistake. You don't wash ties. I came home to a ball of fabric that just couldn't be fixed. She felt so bad for wrecking my ties that she almost cried. I couldn't help but laugh. They looked terrible but I thanked her for trying and threw them all away.

The following year I was moved to the night baker position in the White House. A job that I loved. I would still travel but I loved going in on the afternoons instead of at five in the morning. I then had to shift working for Russell to the mornings and lunches, which worked out well since he gave me more hours and more responsibility. We had a great time working together and I really enjoyed the foods I was working with. I didn't mind cleaning eight cases of squab or gutting fish. It was a labor of love.

Being the night baker meant I would work by myself and create my own dessert menus. I made dinner rolls every night using the old shipboard recipe from the AFRS recipe system and one I was very familiar with. Senior Chief Smith considered it the best bread recipe available. I would make them into sailor's knots and garnish half with sesame seeds and half with poppy seeds.

I did all my own pastry work as well as start to make my own sorbets. I was having fun baking again, something I had forgotten how much I missed. The aroma of fresh bread would hypnotize me. I could never get enough of it. The ability to create something so beautiful from some flour, yeast and water amazed me. I would always hope the people in the dining room would appreciate the breads as much as I did when dropped at their table to tie them over while waiting for their order to be prepared and carried out with extreme care.

Working for President Clinton was more enjoyable that what I could have wished for. When he got voted in it seemed as though nobody knew what to expect but he came to the White House as a breath of fresh air.

His staff was young and looked as if they all just graduated from college. Mr. Clinton had a reputation for liking food, although not the kind of stuff we were doing but rather the kind from fast food restaurants.

We would always listen to the jokes from people while traveling when they heard we were the chefs. "Did you bring the secret sauce for his Big Mac," followed by laughs as if it's the first time we heard that. I guess you take the good with the bad but I would always get annoyed at people trying to be funny about how someone eats. It's not funny, in my opinion.

"So what, he likes burgers. Big deal. Now move along so I can get to work and you could go to the comedy shack on open mike night," is exactly what I really wanted to say to the funny guys.

President Clinton just plain loved food. There is absolutely nothing wrong with that. His eyes would light up when you'd be on

185

the road with him and bring him in some food that he would never get the chance to eat at the function he attended due to people talking to him the whole time.

He would ask, "What's this?" with excitement in his voice as he'd posture up in his chair ready to get stuck in at the word go.

He loved nacho chips and salsa in the hotels he'd stay at. He loved tuna fish sandwiches, french fries and just about everything you and I would like. He was never pretentious about his food and never intimidated by what you put in front of him.

Our kitchen was right next to the Situation Room, where he would spend a lot of time, and he would always come over to visit and see what we were doing. He would reach into the french fry bin and grab some for the road after asking every one of us how we were doing and how our families were. He loved coming to visit.

He would make his rounds as if our votes counted. Look you in the eye and remember where he saw you last. That always made the guys feel special. His eye for detail was as sharp as an eagle's and he would always smirk or wink, lifting up the fries as he walked back to running a country and the largest free enterprise of the world.

Mrs. Clinton was no different. She was always kind to me and I have never found her to be the way she was portrayed in the press. She was cordial and pleasant.

The First Lady wanted to start changing her diet after being on board a few months and switched to vegetarian meals for lunch. I, of course, took charge of making these for her. One day, after making her a marinated grilled vegetable dish with couscous and cardamom candied parsnips with a side of marinated olives and flatbreads, we got a call down to the kitchen from the First Lady's secretary. She wanted to let whomever made Mrs. Clinton's lunch that day to put that dish on the menu permanently. It was one of the greatest compliments I ever received while working there.

Another compliment was when I was the night baker and working lunch at the Blair House. I got a call from Senior Chief Smith sounding in a panic. I was worried something was wrong at home. Turned out the President wanted a salmon dish I made the week previous. The guys needed to know how to make it. I gave him instructions over the phone as if talking to an inexperienced pilot who's trying to land a plane he was at the controls of, and the lives of the passengers depended on my instructions:

Mix some self rising flour with chili powder, salt white pepper and paprika then dredge the salmon filet in it. Sauté the salmon in a little bit of oil and fresh sliced garlic. While the salmon is being sautéed, in a separate pan, sauté five peeled and blanched new potatoes until brown then add chicken stock to cook fondant style. When the salmon gets crispy, turn over to finish the other side. DO NOT OVERCOOK. In a plate, put down a bed of fresh picked spinach, escarole and Belgian endive. Drizzle with some balsamic glaze. Add sliced sweet peppers and onions to the potato pan and taste so the stock doesn't get too salty. Place the salmon on top of the greens. Arrange the potatoes around the salmon then pour the pan jus liquid and peppers over salmon. Garnish with the candied sliced jalapenos and some sweet and spicy chutney. Viola, serve it up.

This was quite a compliment to have made a dish that someone craves, especially the President of the United States. That's what it is all about, in my opinion. I think we are all in the crave business in order to compete with everybody else who does the same thing.

One day I got off early, around two in the afternoon from the Blair House, and I didn't have to bake that night because a holiday was the next day. I was exhausted and looking forward to being home with my family for a nice relaxing night at home. I was sitting on the couch with my oldest son David and trying hard to stay awake. Christina made some coffee and we were having a nice afternoon at home when all of a sudden the phone rang. I was afraid it was work with the normal instructions of "grab your suitcase and head to Andrews." I was happily surprised that it wasn't. It was Sean's parents over from Ireland on holiday and they were in DC looking for me. They wanted a tour of the White House before heading back home.

I politely told them that I would be there in an hour and Christina and the kids went with me. I couldn't believe I was headed back to the city, but for Sean I would have happily gone in the middle of the night.

We arrived at the Ellipse, which is a park behind the White House. I met Sean's Mum and Dad at the south gate and they had their niece Julie with them as well. I did the usual protocol with Secret Service to get them their passes as well as one for my wife. It was around six in the evening and since I couldn't take them to see the Oval Office until eight, I showed them around the OEOB and then into the press room before heading down to the kitchen where I worked. We sat around drinking some iced tea while they admired the decor and I grabbed some M&Ms, menus and other souvenirs for them to take home before it was time to see the Oval Office.

I always got a kick out of being able to show people the Oval Office. It's really quite surreal when you actually see the most famous room in the world. Sean's family were loving it and just like everyone else who sees it, amazed at how small it really is.

As we headed out the West Wing door, Al Gore's limo was at the ready and the Secret Service said he was about to leave. I asked if they wanted to wait and see Al Gore and everybody got excited. As the Vice President came out, my wife Christina approached him with Julie in tow and a menu from the dining room. Christina went on to say how Julie came all the way from Ireland to see him and if he would sign her menu? He immediately obliged. Christina had cut off his Secret Service in order to get to him and I think she caught them off guard. She even asked to keep his pen once he wrote a nice greeting to Julie on the menu. I think it helped when she commented on how tan he looked as well as let him know he looked better in person. After shaking everyone's hands and being whisked away, they stood there in disbelief. It was great. The Willis clan was on cloud nine that night and I was glad to be a part of that.

When I look back upon my time at the White House, I think a lot of what brought me there. It was more than not knowing how to iron; it was a will and determination to be successful that I cannot explain where it came from. I was never brought up in a house of love nor a house of plenty. My road was a rough one but I always looked at it as one that should get smooth with time. Maybe it only gets smooth when more people are on it and I know I wasn't alone in my most challenging moments.

The most influential people in my life are people whom I thought I would never have expected to meet. But we did and I am glad we did.

My wife Christina endured a lot in my quest for perfection. She gave birth to our first born without me there and never questioned why. She raised two beautiful boys to the very best of her ability without me there most of the time and still never asked why. She put up with the phone calls pulling me from home to locations I couldn't reveal and never asked why. She is a pillar of support for me in a profession that always takes me away from her comfort and never asked why.

When I finally decided to leave the Navy, I went home. I went to Scotland.

It was long overdue and I came to find out my timing could not be more perfect. There was a food revolution going on in Scotland. Chef's were working with the local farmers and finding a whole world of bountiful produce available. Angus beef was taking off and becoming a trend. Line-caught fish and sustainable farming were all on trend. It was electric.

Finally Scotland was becoming known for its food and I wanted in on the action.

# ABOUT THE AUTHOR

David T. Macfarlane is a consummate professional chef with influences from Italian culinary passion and Japanese culinary perfection. He shares these influences as he takes Scottish cuisine to the world's stage.

Chef Macfarlane was born in Elderslie, Scotland, and raised in East Kilbride until the age of 10. At age 10, his family moved to the US where David would develop a desire to become a chef.

Upon completion of learning the trade of baking and pastry arts, chef Macfarlane joined the US Navy in an effort to develop his skills further in savory cookery.

Chef Macfarlane spent ten years on active service in the Navy, serving two four-star admirals, the crew and officers of the USS Mount Whitney LCC-20 and the President of the United States in the White House and Blair House in Washington DC.

He is a recipient of many awards and commendations in recognition of his service to the United States, its citizens and its President as a top Navy chef.

David is married, with two children.

CPSIA information can be obtained
at www.ICGtesting.com
Printed in the USA
BVHW03s0152160918
527605BV00001B/4/P

9 780983 236375